CONTENTS

1

INTRODUCTION: SETTING THE STAGE FOR ETSY SUCCESS

Overview of the book and what readers can expect to learn

Welcome to Etsy Business Mastery: A Step-by-Step Guide to Selling Handmade Crafts and Digital Products on Etsy, Including SEO Tips and Strategies. This book is intended to serve as a thorough instruction manual for anyone looking to launch or expand an Etsy business. This book is filled with practical advice that will help you succeed on Etsy, whether you're an expert seller or a total newcomer.

You will discover all the information you require to launch and develop a successful Etsy business throughout this book. Setup of your store, product development and research, photography and product presentation, marketing and promotion, and many other topics will be covered. Furthermore, we will delve into cutting-edge tactics for boosting sales, overcoming difficulties, and scaling your business.

Understanding your target customer and how to use that information to optimize your pricing and product offerings are some of the key things you can expect to learn from this book. We will also go over how to use cross-selling and upselling to raise average order value as well as how to use analytics and data to make wise business decisions.

The emphasis on usability and actionability that this book places on is another crucial aspect. Step-by-step instructions, checklists, and templates are provided throughout the book to assist you in putting the advice and tactics discussed into practice. We think that doing is the best way to learn, so we want to give you the tools and resources you need to get started and start getting results.

We also recognize that operating a business can be difficult, which is why we've included a chapter on overcoming difficulties. We will discuss typical difficulties experienced by Etsy sellers in this chapter and offer solutions. Additionally, we'll go over the significance of managing stress and burnout and offer advice on how to keep a positive outlook and stay motivated.

This book is designed to be a comprehensive guide for anyone looking to start or grow an Etsy business. By the end of this book, you will have a solid understanding of the key concepts and strategies needed to achieve success on Etsy and you will have the tools and resources to take action and see results. We hope that this book will serve as a valuable resource for you on your journey to Etsy success.

Understanding the potential of the Etsy platform and how to leverage it for financial success

Etsy offers manufacturers and small business owners amazing chances to sell their goods to clients all around the world through its marketplace. There are more than 2.7 million active vendors and more than 60 million active shoppers on Etsy. With statistics like those, it is obvious that Etsy is a strong platform with lots of opportunity for financial success.

Knowing your target market is one of the most important things you can do to improve Etsy's chances of being financially successful. It's critical to comprehend who and what your target market is seeking for because the Etsy audience is diverse and international. Knowing your target market will help you make more informed adjustments to your pricing, product offers, and marketing methods.

Utilizing the built-in analytics and tools is another method to take advantage of Etsy's potential. You may utilize Etsy's tools and analytics to comprehend customer behavior better and make data-driven decisions. You can learn a lot about your sales, your clientele's demographics, and other things by using these tools. With this information, you can select the goods to carry, the promotions to run, and the marketing tactics to concentrate on.

Utilizing the in-built marketing and promotion tools is another crucial step in realizing Etsy's full potential. Create a shop announcement, use tags, keywords, and categories to boost visibility, work with bloggers and influencers, and utilize other Etsy services to advertise your store and goods. Utilizing these capabilities will help you raise the exposure of your shop and its products as well as the traffic to your listings. You may increase sales and expand your audience by implementing SEO, email marketing, and social media methods.

Developing a devoted customer base is a critical strategy for realizing Etsy's potential. You may build a devoted clientele that will support your company by offering top-notch customer service, establishing a positive brand image, and encouraging a feeling of community. Repeat business, favorable evaluations, and word-of-mouth advertising may result from this, all of which may contribute to the expansion and success of your company.

The last, but certainly not least, is to keep in mind that Etsy is always getting better. It's critical for sellers to stay current on marketplace changes, platform updates, new features, and industry trends. This might assist you in preserving your competitive advantage and expanding your firm.

On the Etsy marketplace, there is a ton of room for financial success. On Etsy, there are several strategies to prosper and expand your business, including by comprehending your target market, utilizing built-in analytics and tools, utilizing built-in promotion and marketing features, developing a strong customer base, and staying up to date with developments and trends.

Setting realistic goals and creating a plan for achieving them

Without specific objectives that can be measured, it can be challenging to keep track of your progress and make wise business decisions.

Furthermore, establishing improbable goals can result in disappointment and demotivation. Setting attainable goals within a given timeframe and goals that are realistically aligned with your business vision are therefore crucial.

Identifying your company's overall vision is one of the first steps in goal-setting. This should be a succinct, clear statement that captures what you want to accomplish with your company. Developing a community of devoted customers, reaching a specific level of income, or becoming the leading seller in your niche are a few examples of visions.

You can start establishing precise, quantifiable, and doable goals once you have a clear vision for your company. Your overall vision should be reflected in these objectives, which should also be divided into more manageable steps. For instance, your specific objective might be to increase sales by 20% over the next six months if your vision is to become a leading seller in your niche. You could use smaller objectives like enhancing your product photography, growing your social media audience, or introducing a new product line to help you realize this one.

It's crucial to set objectives that you can achieve within the time frame allotted. Setting impossible-to-achieve goals that cannot be completed in the allotted time can cause disappointment and demotivation. Instead of setting larger, more improbable goals that will be challenging to achieve, it is preferable to set smaller, more attainable goals that you can consistently work toward.

Another crucial step is coming up with a strategy for achieving your objectives. This strategy should outline specific tasks and checkpoints that will aid in your goal-achieving. A timeline, a list of the necessary resources, as well as roles and responsibilities, should all be included in the plan. Additionally, it's crucial to regularly assess and monitor your progress so you can adjust as necessary and change your course.

You can track your progress, make wise decisions, and promptly reach your business goals by outlining a clear vision, setting precise, quantifiable, and achievable goals, and developing a comprehensive plan for achieving them. Keep in mind that it is preferable to set smaller, more manageable goals that you can consistently work toward than to set larger, more ambitious ones that will be challenging to achieve.

Understanding the history and growth of Etsy as a marketplace

Founded in 2005 by Robert Kalin, Chris Maguire, and Haim Schoppik, Etsy is an online market place. The business began as a marketplace for handcrafted things but quickly developed a reputation as a source for distinctive and one-of-a-kind goods. The largest and best-known e-commerce site in the world, Etsy, currently boasts 2.7 million active sellers and over 60 million active buyers.

When Kalin, Maguire, and Schoppik collaborated as designers and carpenters in the early 2000s, Etsy was born. They observed a need in the industry for a platform that could link makers of handcrafted goods with consumers seeking out distinctive and one-of-a-kind products. They introduced Etsy in 2005 as a platform for selling handcrafted goods made by craftsmen.

Etsy began as a small maker and consumer marketplace but quickly rose to prominence. Over 150,000 people had registered on the platform by 2007 and it had earned over $4.3 million. By 2009, Etsy had more than 7 million registered members and generated more than $180 million in yearly sales since it received its first round of venture capital funding.

Etsy went public in 2012 and started trading on the stock exchange as its fame grew even more. More than 1.5 billion goods were listed on Etsy in 2015. More than 60 million customers and 2.7 million sellers were utilizing the site by 2020.

A cutting-edge internet marketplace called Etsy brings together manufacturers of handcrafted goods and consumers looking for unusual and distinctive products. The platform also sells a wide variety of commodities in addition to handcrafted goods, such as used and vintage goods, craft materials, and digital downloads. Furthermore, the business has grown to currently offer a variety of services, including shipping labels, online checkout, and Etsy's own payment option.

Since its founding in 2005, Etsy has advanced significantly. It has developed into a global market with millions of active buyers and sellers from a small community of manufacturers and consumers. The platform's success may be credited to both its particular emphasis on handcrafted and one-of-a-kind products and to its dedication to supporting a community of creators and customers. Etsy has established a reputation as a go-to resource for designers and small business owners interested in selling their products online as one of the top e-commerce sites in the world.

Identifying the different types of products that sell well on Etsy and how to find your niche

With a vast selection of goods for sale, Etsy is a diverse marketplace. Understanding the many product categories that do well on Etsy and how to discover your specialty are crucial skills for sellers. This will assist you in choosing the items and market segments that are most likely to be successful for your company.

Handmade goods are one of the most well-liked categories on Etsy. This covers things like jewelry, clothes, home furnishings, and accessories. Because they provide a special and personalized touch that can't be found in mass-produced things, handmade goods are popular on Etsy. Most vendors in this category are craftsmen and craftspeople who produce one-of-a-kind, distinctive goods.

The vintage and used goods section of Etsy is another well-liked section. This includes collectibles, antique furniture, and vintage apparel. These products are well-liked because they provide a distinct and genuine feeling that is unavailable in brand-new products. Buyers who enjoy nostalgia and history find vintage things interesting because they have a past and a backstory.

Digital goods including printable patterns, digital art, and artifacts are another expanding category on Etsy. Because they are simple to manufacture and can be downloaded and printed by the consumer, these goods are well-liked. Additionally, they can save the seller time and money because they don't need physical inventory or delivery.

On Etsy, the category for craft supplies is also very popular. Items like yarn, textiles, beads, and patterns fall within this category. Crafters and DIY lovers who want distinctive, high-quality supplies to make their own creations are fond of these products.

It's crucial to start by figuring out your abilities, hobbies, and areas of enthusiasm while trying to locate your niche. This will enable you to produce goods that thrill you and are consistent with your personal brand. You should also think about how you can set yourself apart from other sellers and the competition in your niche.

Understanding your target market and conducting market research are also crucial. Analyzing customer demographics, keeping an eye on industry trends and top-selling products, being adaptable and open to change, and being prepared to adjust your product offers as necessary are all important.

You may find products that are in demand and target the proper market by knowing the popular categories and conducting market research. Additionally, by trying new things and testing the market, you may learn a lot about the kinds of products that appeal to consumers and change your product lineup accordingly. As your business expands, keep in mind to be loyal to your talents and passions and to be adaptable and open to change.

Understanding the importance of branding and how it can set you apart from the competition

Your company's distinctive brand is what makes it stand out from the competitors. Making a logo is only one aspect of branding; another is developing a unified image and message that appeals to your target market while reflecting the character and values of your company.

Making a distinctive and memorable logo is one of the key components of branding. Your brand's visual identity, represented by your logo, should be straightforward, memorable, and simple to understand. A great logo should convey the essence of your company's identity and be simple to recognize across a variety of platforms and media.

Establishing a consistent image and message throughout all of your marketing assets, such as your website, social media profiles, and packaging, is another crucial component of branding. This entails employing the same colors, typefaces, and graphics throughout all platforms, as well as delivering the same message and core values. Customers will find it simpler to recognize your company and products as a result, helping to build a strong and recognizable brand image.

In branding, consistency is essential since it fosters confidence and trust among your target audience. Customers are more likely to return to and refer your store when your brand is consistent since it fosters reliability and trust.

Making a distinctive and memorable brand name and tagline is another aspect of branding. Your company may stand out from the competition with a distinctive and memorable brand name and tagline, which also helps people remember and locate your store.

The creation of a distinctive and memorable consumer experience is a key component of branding. This includes offering top-notch customer service, developing a positive perception of your business, and encouraging a feeling of community among your clientele. You can build a devoted customer base that will support your company by offering a satisfying customer experience.

Through branding, you may distinguish yourself from the competition, establish credibility with your audience, and develop a distinctive and memorable image. You can develop a strong brand image that connects with your target audience and supports the expansion of your business by developing a distinctive and memorable logo, using consistent colors, fonts, and imagery, coming up with a distinctive and memorable brand name and tagline, and offering a distinctive and memorable customer experience. Keep in mind that branding is a continuous process, so it's crucial to periodically examine and update your branding materials to make sure they remain consistent with your company's vision and values.

Tips for staying organized and motivated as you build your Etsy business

It can be difficult and time-consuming to build a business, and it's simple to become distracted. However, you can stay on course, accomplish your objectives, and establish a flourishing Etsy business by remaining organized and driven.

Making a timetable and adhering to it is one of the most crucial organizational techniques. This should account for the time needed to develop and sell products, handle orders and customer service, and market your company. You may make sure you're using your time wisely and moving closer to your objectives by setting a timetable.

Maintaining a tidy and organized workstation is a crucial component of keeping organized. You'll be able to focus better and work harder as a result. Maintain order and cleanliness on your computer, phone, and in the places where you keep your tools and materials.

Additionally, it's crucial to monitor your development and often set targets. You'll be able to observe how far you've come and maintain your motivation as a result. Setting manageable, short-term objectives that are consistent with your larger vision can keep you motivated and engaged. You can also alter and change course as necessary by constantly analyzing and tracking your progress.

Having a pleasant and encouraging community around you is another way to stay motivated. A network of like-minded people who comprehend the difficulties of starting a business may offer you invaluable support, counsel, and encouragement. This can be a neighborhood networking organization, an online forum, or even a mentor who can help you while you work through the difficulties of starting your own business.

Additionally, it's critical to look after your physical and emotional well-being if you want to maintain your motivation. This covers obtaining adequate rest, eating appropriately, and maintaining an active lifestyle. In addition, remember to take regular pauses and engage in enjoyable hobbies like reading or watching a movie. You'll be able to recharge your batteries and maintain your motivation and attention as a result.

You can stay focused, accomplish your goals, and develop a prosperous Etsy business by making a routine, keeping your workspace tidy and organized, setting frequent goals, surrounding yourself with positive and encouraging people, taking care of yourself, and regularly tracking your progress. Always remain optimistic and remember to recognize your accomplishments along the way.

Preview of the key concepts and strategies that will be covered throughout the book

We'll be delving into a variety of topics in this book that will enable you to maximize and develop your Etsy business. Here's a little peek at what you can discover:

- Understanding your target customer: You must have a thorough awareness of your target market's needs in order to successfully market and sell your products on Etsy. We'll talk about ways to collect client data and use it to develop specialized marketing strategies.
- Optimizing pricing: Pricing is an essential element of every successful business, and this is true of Etsy as well. We'll talk about how to test and experiment to find the right price point for your goods.
- Leveraging upselling and cross-selling: One of the best techniques to increase your profits on Etsy is to raise the average order value. To assist you in doing this, we'll discuss some upselling and cross-selling strategies.
- Utilizing data and analytics: A powerful tool for making wise business decisions is data. We'll discuss how to leverage data and analytics to streamline your pricing, marketing, and advertising initiatives in this book.
- Expanding your business: After starting a profitable Etsy business, you might want to think about branching out to other platforms or even starting your own website. To help you take this next step, we'll give advice and resources.
- Building relationships: Networking and forming connections with other Etsy vendors and subject matter experts may be a great source of assistance and motivation. We'll go over advice for connecting with others and fostering bonds within the Etsy community.

- Staying ahead of the competition: Any market will experience competition, and Etsy is no exception. We'll talk about the value of innovation and how to keep one step ahead of your rivals in the rapidly changing world of e-commerce.

Throughout the book, we'll also be sharing practical tips, case studies, and resources to help you implement the strategies we cover. So whether you're a seasoned Etsy seller or just getting started, this book has something for everyone. So buckle up, and let's get started on the journey to Etsy success!

A call-to-action for readers to take the first step towards Etsy success by setting their own goals.

Setting your personal goals is a crucial first step as you start along the path to Etsy success. Setting definite, quantifiable, and achievable goals can give you a path to achievement and keep you motivated and concentrated.

We want you to take some time to consider your goals for your Etsy business as a reader of this article. Do you want to earn money full-time or are you just trying to augment your existing income? Do you wish to concentrate on a certain market segment or product line? Whatever your objectives, be sure they are measurable, reasonable, and specific.

It's crucial to develop a strategy for reaching your goals after you've set them. This strategy should outline the precise steps and benchmarks you'll need to reach your objectives. For instance, if you want to earn $10,000 per month on Etsy, your strategy might involve listing more products, developing a marketing plan, and contacting influencers in your field.

We are aware that making a strategy and setting goals can seem intimidating, but keep in mind that it's crucial to begin small. Set smaller, more manageable goals for yourself and concentrate on taking one step at a time. Keep in mind that creating a successful Etsy business takes time and work, but with a solid strategy in place and a will to succeed, you can succeed.

We urge you to stop and think about what you want to accomplish, then set attainable, measurable objectives and make a plan to get there. Always remember to start small, to stay on task, and to persevere in your endeavors. We are here to support you every step of the way because we have faith in your potential to succeed.

2

SETTING UP YOUR ETSY SHOP: THE BASICS

Choosing a shop name and creating a brand

Making a solid first impression is crucial since potential clients will see your shop name and brand initially.

A few crucial elements should be taken into account while picking a shop name. Your store's name should be simple to remember and spell, first. Customers will have an easier time finding and remembering your store if it has a catchy, memorable name. Furthermore, it's crucial to pick a shop name that appropriately describes the goods and services you provide. This will make it simpler for customers to find what they're looking for and will help them understand what your store is all about.

The time has come to start building your brand after selecting a shop name. Your brand is the overarching perception and idea you wish to give customers. Things like your logo, colors, and typeface fall under this category. Your brand should be the same on all channels, including your website, social media accounts, and Etsy store.

Targeting your audience when developing your brand is crucial. What kinds of goods and services are they looking for? What kind of picture or message elicits a response from them? You can develop a brand that resonates with your target market and increases the likelihood that they will become customers by knowing who they are.

The development of a consistent client experience is also crucial. This covers everything like how you interact with consumers, how your products are packaged and shipped, and how your shop looks and feels overall. You can encourage your consumers' trust and loyalty by providing a consistent customer experience.

It takes time and work to build a powerful brand, but it's worthwhile. Your store will stand out, draw in new consumers, and develop a devoted following if you have a strong brand. Always put your consumers first, be consistent, and hold true to your ideals.

Making a solid first impression is crucial since potential clients will see your shop name and brand initially. Create a powerful brand that resonates with your target demographic and offers a consistent customer experience, together with a memorable and reflected shop name. Be aware that developing a brand requires time and work, but with perseverance and patience, you will be able to construct a brand that will set you apart from the competitors and support the growth of your Etsy business.

Setting up shop policies and payment methods

These procedures and rules will provide clients a clear understanding of what to anticipate when buying from you, which will increase client trust and confidence in your company.

It's crucial to take the following factors into account while creating shop policies:

- Shipping and handling policies: This must to contain details regarding your policy on returns and exchanges, as well as delivery estimates and charges.
- Payment methods: Information on the many payment alternatives you accept, such as credit cards, PayPal, and other online payment choices, should be included.

- Refund and return policies: This should contain details on what clients might anticipate if they want to exchange or return a product.
- Privacy policy: This should contain details about your plans for using the personal data of your clients and safeguarding their privacy.
- Legal notices: any legal notices, such a disclaimer or terms of use, that are mandated by your jurisdiction.

Additionally, it's crucial to guarantee that your policies are simple to locate and comprehend. They have to be easily visible to customers and publicly placed in your store.

It's crucial to give your customers a range of options when it comes to payment methods. They will find it easier to buy from you because of this, and more sales will result as well. Credit cards, PayPal, and other online payment alternatives are some of the most used payment methods on Etsy. Additionally, it's critical to guarantee the security of your payment processes and the privacy of your customers' financial and personal data.

Policies safeguard the security of customers' personal and financial information and give them clear information about what to expect from your organization. They also serve to foster customer trust and confidence. You may enhance sales by making it easier for clients to make purchases by offering a range of payment alternatives.

Understanding the different listing options and setting prices

While the incorrect listing options and prices may drive away customers, the proper ones might assist draw clients and boost sales.

Etsy gives merchants a variety of choices when it comes to listing options. These consist of:

- Listing your product for a set price: The simplest listing choice, this one works best for items with constant prices.

- Listing your product for a custom price: This choice works well for items that come in a variety of pricing ranges, including custom-made or one-of-a-kind products.
- Listing your product as a digital download: Digital goods like e-books, digital art, or music are ideally suited for this alternative.
- Listing your product as a service: For services like consulting, graphic design, or photography, this choice is the finest.

It's critical to take into account the cost of your raw materials, the time and effort required to make your product, and the level of competition in your market when determining prices. You should also take into account the value your product provides to the customer and the price they are prepared to pay.

Remember to set competitive prices for your goods as well. This implies that your prices should be competitive with those of comparable goods in your market. Pricing your goods competitively will help you draw in more people and boost sales.

Being adaptable and modifying prices as necessary is another crucial component of pricing. This might entail providing discounts and promotions, or changing prices in response to market fluctuations or client feedback.

While the incorrect listing options and prices may drive away customers, the proper ones might assist draw clients and boost sales. It's crucial to think about the cost of your supplies, the time and effort it takes to make your product, the competition in your market, the value your product provides to the customer, and set a competitive pricing for your goods. Furthermore, being adaptable and raising pricing as necessary will help you maintain your competitiveness and boost sales.

Optimizing your shop for search and visibility

Making your store easy to find and ensuring that potential customers can view your merchandise will help you increase sales and grow your company.

One of the most important methods to increase the exposure of your store and visibility for searches is search engine optimization (SEO). In order for potential buyers to locate your products on Etsy or on other search engines like Google, you must include keywords in your product descriptions, tags, and names. It is crucial to carry out research on the keywords that your target customers would likely use to find products similar to yours and to include those keywords in your product listings.

Using high-quality product photographs is an essential part of enhancing your store's exposure and search rankings. The best lighting should be used to clearly show off your products in your product shots. Make sure your photos are optimized for the website and the right size, resolution, and quality for the web.

You could increase the visibility and search rankings of your store by marketing your products on social media and other platforms. This can involve creating a social media plan, advertising advertisements, and collaborating with influencers in your area of expertise. Making a website for your Etsy business and optimizing it for SEO is a great way to increase visibility and draw customers to it.

Another tactic to increase visibility is to take part in Etsy's sponsored listings and advertisements program. You can increase the audience for your listings and raise the exposure of your platform with the aid of this program.

Making your store easy to find and ensuring that potential customers can view your merchandise will help you increase sales and grow your company. Important steps toward achieving this include employing keywords in your product listings, taking professional photos, promoting your products on social media and other platforms, building a website, and participating in Etsy's promoted listings and ads program.

Setting up your shop policies, shipping, and taxes

Shop policies, shipping options and tax regulations will provide customers with clear information about what they can expect when making a purchase from your shop and it will also help you to comply with the legal requirements.

It's critical to provide your customers with a range of delivery options. They will find it easier to buy from you because of this, and more sales will result as well. Standard shipping, expedited delivery, and international shipping are some of the most common shipping options. Additionally, make sure your shipping options are reasonable and your products are wrapped and transported in a way that will guarantee their safe arrival.

Taxes are another crucial consideration when opening your business. It's critical to comprehend the tax regulations that apply to your company because they vary by state and country. To learn more about the tax regulations that relate to you, you should speak with a tax expert or visit the website of your local government.

Making it easier for clients to make a purchase will enhance sales if you offer a number of delivery options and are aware of your tax obligations.

Creating a shop banner and logo that represents your brand

Making a solid first impression is crucial since potential consumers will see your business banner and logo right away when they enter. A professionally created banner and logo can draw in customers and increase company recognition.

It's crucial to take the following factors into account while making a shop banner:

- Use high-quality images: Your banner should be visually stunning and effectively represent your products or company. Use clear, well-lit, high-resolution photographs that present your goods or brand in an appealing, expert manner.
- Keep it simple: Limit the amount of text or images you use in your banner. Potential clients will be more drawn to a design that is straightforward and appealing.

- Use your brand colors: Create a unified look and feel by using the colors from your branding and logo in your banner.
- Use a call-to-action: Use a call-to-action to entice people to interact with your store, such as "Shop Now" or "Explore our products."

It's crucial to take the following factors into account while designing a logo:

- Keep it simple: A simple logo is easier to remember and recognize than a complex one.
- Use vector graphics: Without sacrificing quality, vector graphics can be scaled to any size. This is crucial when creating a logo for use on your website, business cards, and packaging, among other places.
- Use your brand colors: To create a consistent look and feel, incorporate the colors from your branding into your logo.
- Make it versatile: Your logo should be adaptable to different backgrounds and look good in both color and black and white.
- Hire a professional designer: Consider working with a professional graphic designer to create a logo for your brand if you're unsure of your design abilities.

When a potential customer walks into your shop, your shop banner and logo will be the first thing they see, so it's critical to make a strong first impression. Customers can be drawn in and brand trust can be increased with the use of a well-designed banner and logo. Utilize call-to-actions, high-quality graphics, your brand's colors, and keep your banner and logo basic. To build a logo that professionally portrays your brand, you should also think about employing a qualified graphic designer.

Understanding the importance of good customer service and how to handle customer inquiries

While bad customer service might turn away clients, good customer service can help you gain their confidence and loyalty.

Consider the following when providing excellent customer service:

- Be prompt: Be as prompt as you can in your responses to customer questions. By doing this, you will increase client trust and demonstrate your respect for their time.
- Be friendly: In each and every one of your interactions with customers, be kind and professional. This will facilitate the development of a solid rapport with your clients.
- Be helpful: Customers should receive accurate and useful information. By doing so, you will increase trust and demonstrate your subject-matter expertise.
- Be proactive: Take the initiative to foresee and respond to client problems before they escalate into issues.

It's crucial to take into account the following when responding to consumer inquiries:

- Listen:Pay attention to your customer's issues and make an effort to comprehend them. This will enable you to offer them a better fix for their issue.
- Apologize: If the client's complaint is justified, apologise and accept responsibility for the issue.
- Offer a solution: Provide a remedy that will take care of the client's issue.
- Follow up: Verify that the customer's issue has been remedied by following up with them.
- Document: Keep track of client enquiries and the actions taken in response. You can use this moving forward to enhance your client service.

While bad customer service might turn away clients, good customer service can help you gain their confidence and loyalty. When interacting with consumers, be on time, amiable, accommodating, and proactive. In order to enhance your customer service moving forward, you should also listen, apologize, offer a solution, follow up, and document client inquiries and how they were handled.

Tips for creating an easy checkout process

A simple checkout procedure can boost revenue and raise client happiness.

It's crucial to take the following factors into account when designing a simple checkout process:

- Keep the process simple: Keep the checkout procedure as straightforward as you can. Make sure the process is simple to follow and avoid requesting unneeded information.
- Offer a variety of payment options: Provide a range of payment choices, including credit card, PayPal, and additional online payment options. Customers will find it more convenient to buy as a result.
- Keep shipping costs clear: Make sure the checkout process includes a clear statement of the shipping charges. Customers will be better able to comprehend the full cost of their purchase as a result, increasing the likelihood that they will finish the transaction..
- Provide a Guest Checkout option: Allow customers to check out as a guest, so they don't have to create an account to make a purchase.

A simple checkout procedure can boost revenue and enhance customer happiness. To make the process more convenient for customers and raise the likelihood that they will complete a purchase, offer a variety of payment options, make shipping costs clear, use a progress indicator, ensure the checkout process is mobile-friendly, include clear calls-to-action, and offer a guest checkout option.

How to set up shop sections to organize your products

Creating divisions for your products makes it simpler for customers to find what they are looking for and may even boost sales.

It's critical to take the following factors into account when putting up shop sections:

- Group similar products together: Organize products into divisions by similarity. You might have an area for jewelry, one for clothing, and one for home décor, for instance.
- Use descriptive titles: For your section titles, be descriptive. You may use "Handmade Leather Accessories" or "Vintage Inspired Jewelry" in place of "Accessories," for instance.
- Use tags: To better arrange your products within each section, use tags. For instance, you might have tags for "necklaces," "bracelets," "earrings," and "rings" under the jewelry area.
- Create sections for new products: Make new product sections to highlight your most recent innovations and give them greater exposure.
- Use sections to promote sales and discounts: To make it simple for clients to find the products that are on sale, use sections to highlight sales and discounts.
- Utilize the feature of "featured sections": Use the "featured sections" function to draw attention to particular products or areas, increasing the likelihood that customers will see them.
- Consider the customer's journey: To increase the chance that buyers will notice certain items or regions, use the "featured sections" tool to draw attention to them.

Use the "featured sections" function to highlight specific products or geographic areas in order to raise the likelihood that customers will pay attention to them.

Overview of the different shop options (Standard, Plus, and Pattern) and their features

Three shop choices are available on Etsy for its sellers: Standard, Plus, and Pattern. Every alternative has a unique combination of characteristics and advantages, so it's critical to comprehend how they differ so you can pick the one that is finest for your company.

Standard:

The entry-level plan provided by Etsy is the Standard shop option. You can offer products for sale without paying any additional listing costs when you start a Standard shop. Basic Etsy capabilities including the ability to post products, handle orders, and communicate with customers are available to standard businesses. Additionally, a variety of tools, including tools for analytics and promotion, inventory management, and shop management, are included.

Plus:

An improved version of the Standard shop is the Plus shop choice. The capacity to sell in numerous languages and currencies, access extensive analytics and promotion tools, and the opportunity to generate unique web addresses are just a few of the extra services that sellers may access for a monthly cost. Additionally, shops have access to more customization choices and the opportunity to design unique shop sections.

Pattern:

The most sophisticated option on Etsy is the Pattern shop. It is intended for vendors that wish to open an Etsy store and their own website. Pattern shops have all the advantages of Plus shops, but they also let sellers build their own websites with unique domains and manage those websites using Etsy's robust e-commerce platform. Additionally, a variety of themes and design options are provided to assist sellers in building a website that reflects their brand and looks professional.

Every alternative has a unique combination of characteristics and advantages, so it's critical to comprehend how they differ so you can pick the one that is finest for your company. Plus shops have access to more features and customization possibilities, while Pattern stores have all the capabilities of Plus shops and additionally let sellers build their own websites with unique domains. Standard shops are free to open and give customers access to Etsy's core functionality.

A guide on how to set up your shop to be compliant with Etsy's policies and regulations

To make sure that all sellers are acting honestly and ethically, Etsy has put in place a set of rules and guidelines. Penalties, such as suspension or closure of your shop, may be imposed for violation of these rules.

It's crucial to keep the following in mind when setting up your shop to comply with Etsy's rules:

- Understand Etsy's policies:Make sure you are familiar with Etsy's policies and what is and isn't permitted on the website. These regulations cover a wide range of topics, including product safety, intellectual property rights, and forbidden products.
- Follow copyright and trademark laws: Verify that all of the things you advertise for sale on Etsy adhere to all applicable trademark and copyright regulations. You shouldn't list fake or knockoff goods and you shouldn't use language or photos that you don't have authorization to use.
- Accurately describe your products: Give a thorough description of your items and include any details that might affect their usage or worth. This provides details about the components utilized, the measurements, and the state of the objects.
- Be honest about shipping times: Make sure you can fulfill orders within the timeframe you advertise and be honest about shipping timeframes.
- Provide accurate and honest feedback: Give honest and accurate feedback on your goods and services.
- Keep records: Keep track of all exchanges and transactions in case there are any complaints or problems later on.

upcoming trends and goods that are likely to become popular in the future.
- Keep an eye on social media trends: Pay attention to social media trends and think about how you may use them to your products and services. Popular social media trends can also serve as a reliable predictor of the kinds of goods that will sell well on Etsy.
- Test different products and niches: Test them by listing a few products in those categories after you've identified a few lucrative markets and product trends. Keep an eye on sales and customer feedback, then modify your strategy as necessary.

Use the search and explore tools on Etsy, the trend reports, keep an eye on social media trends, and test out various products and categories as you research your competition. You can then modify your strategy to take into account the profitable product niches and trends on Etsy.

Conducting market research and understanding customer needs

You may adjust your offers to match the needs of your clients and improve your chances of success by being aware of their needs and desires.

It's crucial to keep the following in mind when performing market research and comprehending customer needs:

- Identify your target market: Investigate the characteristics of your ideal client to determine your target market. Age, gender, economic level, and geography are just a few examples of the data included.
- Understand their needs and wants: By investigating what they are seeking for in items similar to yours, you may better understand the needs and desires of your target market. Information like pricing range, product attributes, and preferred design are included.

- Monitor customer reviews and feedback: Keep an eye on consumer comments and reviews to learn what they like and dislike about
- Use social media and online forums: Use social media and internet forums to learn what your customers want and to keep up with the conversations and trends in your industry.
- Conduct surveys and customer interviews: To receive direct input from customers, conduct surveys and customer interviews. This might offer insightful information about what clients require and want from your items.
- Analyze the data: Look for patterns and trends in the data you gathered throughout your market research by analyzing it. You can use this information to make well-informed judgments regarding your products and marketing tactics.

Choose your target market, ascertain their needs and desires, keep an eye on customer reviews and feedback, utilize social media and online discussion boards, carry out surveys and client interviews, and then analyze the information gathered. By doing this, you may boost your chances of success and make judgments regarding your products and business strategy that are well-informed.

Developing and sourcing products that will sell on Etsy

It's crucial to keep the following things in mind when creating and acquiring goods for Etsy sales:

- Identify profitable niches and product trends: By completing market research, utilizing Etsy's search and explore tools, and keeping an eye on social media trends, you can spot lucrative niches and product trends. This will assist you in determining what goods are in demand and which market sectors are most likely to be lucrative.
- Develop your own products: Utilize your creativity and expertise to create your own items. Generating handmade

goods, designing and printing original artwork, or creating your own patterns are all examples of this.

- Source products from wholesalers: If you lack the resources or expertise to create your own products, buy wholesale products. Find wholesalers who focus on products that are in high demand and that complement your brand and niche.
- Visit trade shows and markets: To find fresh and distinctive things that you can sell on Etsy, visit trade exhibitions and markets. By doing so, you'll be able to identify products that aren't yet publicly available and remain on top of trends.
- Look for unconventional sourcing options: To find one-of-a-kind items you can sell on Etsy, search for nontraditional sources like garage sales, thrift shops, and vintage shops.
- Quality control: Make sure the items in your shop satisfy the requirements for quality and are compliant with Etsy's policies before you offer them.

Discover lucrative market niches and product trends, create your own products, buy wholesale, attend trade fairs and markets, explore for unorthodox sourcing alternatives, and make sure your products match Etsy's quality requirements and rules.

Tips for researching and identifying profitable niches on Etsy

It's crucial to take into account the following advice while looking into and locating lucrative niches on Etsy:

- Use Etsy's search and explore features: Use Etsy's search and exploration tools to find the most sought-after goods and market segments. You may explore the various categories to see what things are trending, or you can use keywords to search for specific products.
- Monitor customer reviews and feedback: To learn what customers like and hate about your items and those of your competitors, keep an eye on customer reviews and feedback.

This can offer insightful information about what goods are in demand and which market sectors are most likely to be lucrative.

- Use Etsy's trend reports: Every month, Etsy publishes a trend report for the website that lists the most well-liked products, fashions, and themes. You can use these reports to discover upcoming trends and goods that are likely to become popular in the future.
- Keep an eye on social media trends: Observe social media trends and think about how you may use them to your services. Popular social media trends can also serve as a reliable predictor of the kinds of goods that will sell well on Etsy.
- Test different products and niches: Test them by listing a few products in those categories after you've identified a few lucrative markets and product trends. Keep an eye on sales and customer feedback, then modify your strategy as necessary.
- Research your competition: Find out what items and markets your rivals are focusing on by doing some research on them. Take a look at the items that are doing well and think of any market gaps you may fill.

Utilize Etsy's search and exploration tools, keep an eye on customer reviews and feedback, use trend reports, follow social media trends, test various products and market segments, and investigate your rivals. You can find the lucrative Etsy niches in this way and change your strategy accordingly.

Understanding the importance of customer research and how to conduct it

It's critical to take into account the following while figuring out the value of consumer research and how to do it:

- Identify your target market: Investigate the characteristics of your ideal client to determine your target market. Age, gender, economic level, and geography are just a few examples of the data included.
- Understand their needs and wants: By investigating what they are seeking for in items similar to yours, you may better understand the needs and desires of your target market. Information like pricing range, product attributes, and preferred design are included.
- Monitor customer reviews and feedback: To learn what customers like and hate about your items and those of your competitors, keep an eye on customer reviews and feedback. This can offer insightful information about the most popular items and features among consumers.
- Use social media and online forums: Use social media and internet forums to learn what your customers want and to keep up with the conversations and trends in your industry.
- Conduct surveys and customer interviews: To receive direct input from customers, conduct surveys and customer interviews. This might offer insightful information about what clients require and want from your items.
- Analyze the data: To find patterns and trends, analyze the data you received from your customer study. You can use this information to make well-informed judgments regarding your products and marketing tactics.

Choose your target market, ascertain their needs and desires, keep an eye on customer reviews and feedback, utilize social media and online discussion boards, carry out surveys and client interviews, and then analyze the information gathered. By doing this, you may improve your chances of success and make judgments regarding your products and business strategy that are well-informed.

How to use data and analytics to identify product trends and customer preferences

It's crucial to take into account the following when using data and analytics to determine product trends and customer preferences:

- Utilize Etsy's analytics: Etsy provides a variety of insights and indicators that can show you how your company is doing, as well as reveal market trends and client preferences. Information like views, favorites, sales, and money are included in this.
- Track your competitors: Utilize tools like Google Analytics and SEMrush to keep tabs on your competitors' traffic, search engine placements, and backlinks. This might assist you in determining the popular items and market segments among your competitors so that you can modify your strategy accordingly.
- Use Google Trends: To find the most common search phrases and trends in your niche, use Google Trends. This can assist you in determining the popular items and search terms so that you can modify your product offers and marketing plans accordingly.
- Analyze customer feedback: Analyze customer feedback by keeping an eye on online reviews, comments on social media, and survey results. This can offer insightful information about what customers value most in terms of features and what they like and dislike about your items.
- Use A/B testing: To test various product listings, prices, and marketing tactics, use A/B testing. This can assist you in figuring out what works best and deciding on your items and corporate plans with knowledge.
- Invest in data analysis tools: To evaluate your data more quickly and accurately, spend money on platforms like Google Analytics, Mixpanel, and Looker.

Make use of Etsy's statistics, keep tabs on your rivals, use Google

Trends, examine customer reviews, conduct A/B testing, and spend money on data analysis tools. By doing so, you may spot market trends and customer preferences and modify your plan as necessary.

Techniques for developing and sourcing new products that align with customer needs

Continuous customer research is a critical strategy for creating and acquiring new items that are in line with consumer demands. This will assist you in staying current with the requirements and desires of your customers, in spotting new product opportunities, and in figuring out what customers want from goods similar to yours.

Utilizing consumer input to guide product development is another crucial strategy. You may learn a lot about the features that customers find most important and the enhancements they would like to see by listening to what they have to say about your goods and those of your rivals. You can produce items that are suited to the requirements of your clients by incorporating customer recommendations into your product development.

Finding market gaps is a different strategy. You can find new product opportunities and create goods that will close those gaps by investigating the items that are currently on the market and those that are missing. Try to develop and enhance current items by giving them new features, making them more environmentally friendly, or both. You can use this to develop new product opportunities and set your items apart from those of your rivals.

Investing in prototyping and testing is crucial if you want to make sure that your products are high-quality and suit your clients' expectations. This will assist you in finding any issues before you release your products and in making any necessary adjustments.

You can identify market gaps, try to innovate and improve current products, invest in prototyping and testing, and continuously conduct customer research to better understand the needs and wants of your customers. By doing this, you can create new product opportunities and make sure that your products satisfy their needs.

Tips for creating a product line that is consistent with your brand and niche

You may build a recognizable brand, draw in and keep customers, and boost revenue with a consistent product line. The following advice will help you develop a product line that is consistent with your brand and market niche:

To start, it's critical to understand your brand and specialty clearly. Establish your brand's vision, core principles, and differentiators, then utilize this information to direct the creation of new products. By investigating the items that are currently on the market and the needs of consumers, you may better understand your niche. This will assist you in finding new product opportunities and creating goods that are consistent with your brand and market niche.

Second, it's crucial to have a unified style and design across your whole product line. This encompasses the hues, designs, compositions, and packaging. As a result, your products will have a consistent look and feel and be simple to recognize. Making a style guide with all the design components you wish to employ consistently will help you do this.

Third, having a consistent pricing plan is crucial. Ensure that your pricing plan is consistent with your market segment and the caliber of your offerings. This will assist you build client trust and make it simpler for them to appreciate the worth of your goods.

Fourth, it's critical to stay within your specialization and abstain from deviating too much from it. Concentrate on developing a limited number of well chosen niche-relevant products. This will assist you in building a strong brand identity and attracting clients that are enthusiastic about your specialized market.

Fifth, it's critical to keep up with developments and modifications in your specialized field. This will assist you in staying current and spotting new business chances. Observe what your rivals are doing and work to keep one step ahead of them.

You can create a recognizable brand, draw in and keep customers, and boost your sales by having a clear understanding of your brand and niche, having a consistent aesthetic and design, having a consistent pricing strategy, sticking to your niche, and staying up to date with trends and changes in your niche.

Understanding the importance of product quality and how to ensure it

The choice of high-quality materials is one of the most crucial factors to take into account while ensuring product quality. Using strong, long-lasting materials that will stand up well over time is part of this. Additionally, make sure that the resources you employ are secure and adhere to any applicable laws.

The quality of your products' construction is a further crucial factor to take into account. Make sure your products are well-made, with an emphasis on finishing and attention to detail. Products that have been properly completed will be more durable and appealing to customers' eyes.

A crucial element in guaranteeing product quality is testing. It is crucial to test new products to ensure they function as intended and are secure before releasing them. Testing for sturdiness, usability, and regulatory compliance can all be a part of this.

Maintaining quality also means making sure that your products are packaged and labeled properly. Your products will be adequately protected throughout storage and transportation. Customers will have access to correct information about your items, including care guidelines and safety precautions, thanks to proper labeling.

Last but not least, it's critical to have a clear and consistent return policy. In the event of any problems, this will serve to safeguard both you and your clients. Make sure your return policy is made clear on your listing and that you address any client complaints or concerns as soon as they arise.

How to create a product development strategy and roadmap

It's crucial to establish a schedule for attaining your goals and to lay forth specific objectives that complement your overall business plan.

By establishing checkpoints along the way, you may monitor progress and make changes as necessary.

For a product development strategy to be effective, detailed market research is essential. You can find new product opportunities, comprehend client wants and preferences, and stay on the cutting edge by researching your target market, rivals, and industry trends.

The aim is to build a productive and efficient product development process. The steps of this procedure should include ideation, prototype, testing, and launch. The process will function smoothly if roles and duties are clearly defined within the team and regular meetings are held to monitor progress.

It's crucial to build a product roadmap outlining the measures you'll take to produce new items. Timelines, benchmarks, and deliverables should all be listed on this roadmap. Along with a plan for launching and scaling your goods, it should also include a strategy for testing and verifying your products.

Making data-driven decisions regarding your product development plan will be easier if you have a system in place for monitoring and assessing product performance. You can modify your approach to make sure it is in line with your objectives by keeping an eye on the performance of your product.

You can stay organized, focused, and on track as you develop new products and expand your business by setting clear goals, conducting in-depth market research, creating an efficient and effective product development process, creating a product roadmap, and having a system in place for tracking and analyzing product performance.

The importance of trademark and copyright when creating new product

The process of legally registering a name, symbol, or design that identifies and sets your products apart from those of others is known as trademarking. By registering your brand name and logo as trademarks, you not only give yourself the legal right to sue anybody who violates your trademark rights but also prevent others from using your brand name and logo without your consent.

The legal defense provided to those who create original works of art, music, and literature is known as copyright. It also holds true for any images and other artistic creations that you utilize in your product listings. You risk being accused of copyright infringement if you use another person's work without their consent.

It's crucial to ensure that you are not violating any current trademarks or copyrights when developing new items. This involves making sure that the names, logos, and designs of your items don't resemble those of other businesses or products that are already on the market. You should refrain from utilizing information or images protected by a copyright in your product listings.

You should also be aware that certain materials, including fabrics, can be covered by design patents. This indicates that the fabric's design is exclusive and cannot be copied without authorization.

You should file for trademark and copyright registrations to safeguard your original works. As a result, you will receive legal protection and be able to file a lawsuit against anyone who violates your rights.

Understanding the significance of trademarks and copyrights gives you legal protection for your original work as well as for your brand and ensures that you are working within the law. You may protect your company and stay out of trouble by making sure your product names, logos, and designs are distinctive from those of competing goods or brands, avoiding utilizing language or images protected by copyright in your product listings, and registering your trademarks and copyrights.

Identifying and sourcing materials and suppliers

For developing and producing high-quality products that can sell well on Etsy, one has to have access to dependable suppliers and high-quality materials. Here are some pointers for locating vendors and materials:

It's crucial to take into account aspects like cost, availability, and quality while choosing materials. Additionally, think about how the products you use will affect the environment and whether they adhere to any applicable laws. Finding the finest solutions for your company can be aided by doing some research on various suppliers and materials.

It's crucial to look for providers who provide premium materials at reasonable pricing while sourcing vendors. Additionally, think about things like minimum order sizes, lead times, and the reputation of the supplier. To guarantee that you obtain dependable and regular service, it's crucial to have strong working relationships with your suppliers.

Meeting potential suppliers and learning about cutting-edge products and trends can both be accomplished through networking and trade fair attendance. A wonderful way to network with other business owners who can offer recommendations for suppliers and materials is to join clubs and forums for your sector.

Understanding the conditions of the agreement, such as payment terms, delivery deadlines, and minimum order quantities, is crucial when working with suppliers. Additionally, it's critical to have a plan for handling any problems and to communicate clearly.

Additionally, it's critical to be aware of and adhere to any applicable regulations relating to materials and suppliers, such as those governing fair trade, import and export, and the environment.

You can make sure that you have access to high-quality materials and dependable suppliers, which will help you develop and produce high-quality products, by taking into account factors like cost, availability, and quality, researching various materials and suppliers, developing a good working relationship with suppliers, networking and attending trade shows, having a clear understanding of the terms of the agreement, and being aware of and adhering to any relevant regulations.

Tips for prototyping and testing new products.

A crucial phase of the product development process is prototyping and testing new items. It enables you to evaluate your items' use, attractiveness, and design before committing to mass production. Here are some pointers for developing and testing prototypes of new products:

When prototyping, it's crucial to start with a straightforward, straightforward prototype that is easy to construct. Before going on to more complicated prototypes, this will enable you to test the fundamental functionality of your product and make any necessary improvements.

To gain a variety of responses, it's crucial to test your prototypes with a varied set of people. This can apply to close friends, relatives, and potential clients. By doing this, you can find any problems with the layout or usability of your product and fix them before starting production.

The design, functionality, and general appeal of the product are just a few examples of the numerous components of the product that should be considered when testing. Additionally, think about the product's use, durability, and prospective target market.

It's crucial to take your product's price and scalability into account. This entails assessing your product's production and material costs as well as its prospective demand.

Additionally, it's crucial to think about your product's safety certifications and standards and make sure it complies with them.

4

PHOTOGRAPHY AND PRODUCT PRESENTATION

Tips for taking and editing high-quality product photos

High-quality product images can help you distinguish yourself from the competition while showcasing your products in the best possible light. The following advice will help you take and edit superior product photos:

To guarantee that your images are well-lit, it's crucial to use natural light or a light box when photographing them. You can avoid shadows and take photos that look more polished by doing this.

To make sure that your images are crystal clear and sharp, it's also crucial to choose a high-resolution camera or smartphone camera. This will enable you to highlight the specifics of your goods and increase its allure to potential customers.

It's crucial to utilize picture editing software like Adobe Lightroom or Photoshop when editing your photos to make changes like cropping, altering the brightness and contrast, and erasing any blemishes or faults.

In order to give your shop a unified look and feel, it's crucial to use the same background and setup for all of your product images.

Using picture editing software is essential for improving the aesthetic and professionalism of your photos. The brightness, contrast, and color balance should all be adjusted as well as any defects or imperfections.

In order to provide your customers a better understanding of what they are buying and to boost the likelihood that they will buy your goods, it is also critical to have many photographs of each product.

Creating compelling product listings with attention-grabbing titles and descriptions

You may enhance sales and draw in more potential customers by writing a compelling product listing. The following advice will help you make engaging product listings with catchy titles and descriptions:

Use keywords that appropriately describe your product and make it simple for people to find your listing while coming up with the title for your goods. To help it stand out from other listings, you should think about making your title interesting and attention-grabbing.

Being brief and clear when creating your product description is crucial. Make it simple for buyers to comprehend what your product is and what it can achieve for them by outlining its essential characteristics in bullet points.

Utilizing top-notch photos that best display your product is also crucial. Customers will be better able to picture your goods thanks to this, which will enhance the likelihood that they'll buy it.

Additionally, you should provide any pertinent information that a potential consumer might want to know, such as size, color, and material characteristics.

Additionally, it's crucial to be truthful and open in your product descriptions. This entails giving precise measurements and details as well as disclosing any flaws or damages.

In order to entice customers to buy your product, it's crucial to include a call-to-action in your product listing.

You can draw in potential customers and boost sales by using keywords that accurately describe your product, creating a catchy and attention-grabbing title, being succinct and clear in your product description, using high-quality images, including relevant details, being honest and transparent, and including a call-to-action.

Optimizing your shop's appearance and branding

You can draw in more consumers, boost sales, and differentiate your business from the competition with the help of a well-designed store and consistent branding. Here are some pointers for improving the look and branding of your store:

It's crucial to design your store with a unified aesthetic that reflects your brand and market niche. Using the same color scheme, typography, and graphics throughout your store can help you achieve this.

Utilizing top-notch visuals and images that best represent your products is also crucial. Customers will be better able to picture your things thanks to this, increasing the likelihood that they'll buy something.

Additionally, it's critical to maintain an orderly and user-friendly shop. If you want to make it easier for customers to locate what they're looking for, you can include a search bar, a clear and straightforward menu, and store sections to arrange your products.

A logo, banner, and "About" page that represent your brand and aid clients in understanding what your store is all about are also essential.

The branding you develop for your shop should be consistent throughout all of its components, including the title, tags, bio, and social network accounts.

Understanding the importance of good product photography and how it can impact sales

High-quality product photography can help you distinguish yourself from the competition while showcasing your products in the best possible light. The following advice will help you comprehend the value of effective product photography and how it might affect sales:

Because it enables clients to imagine your products and comprehend their characteristics and benefits, effective product photography is crucial. Customers may make well-informed purchasing selections with the aid of detailed, high-quality photographs that are well-lit and depict the goods.

Additionally, effective product photography can help to boost client confidence and engagement. The likelihood that a customer will interact with a product listing that features crisp, high-quality photographs is higher. This may raise credibility and boost sales opportunities.

Additionally, effective product photography might help you differentiate yourself from the competitors. Making your products stand out from the competition on Etsy can be challenging. You may draw in more customers and boost sales by using high-quality photos that best represent your products.

To guarantee that your product shots are well-lit, it's crucial to use natural light or a light box when photographing them. You can avoid shadows and take photos that look more polished by doing this.

To make sure that your images are crystal clear and sharp, it's also crucial to choose a high-resolution camera or smartphone camera. This will enable you to highlight the specifics of your goods and increase its allure to potential customers.

It's crucial to utilize picture editing software like Adobe Lightroom or Photoshop when editing your photos to make changes like cropping, altering the brightness and contrast, and erasing any blemishes or faults.

In order to give your shop a unified look and feel, it's crucial to use the same background and setup for all of your product images.

Tips for taking high-quality product photos with a smartphone or camera

High-quality product images can help you distinguish yourself from the competition while showcasing your products in the best possible light. Here are some pointers for capturing excellent product shots using a camera or smartphone:

To guarantee that your product shots are well-lit, it's crucial to use natural light or a light box when photographing them. You can avoid shadows and take photos that look more polished by doing this.

To make sure that your images are crystal clear and sharp, it's also crucial to choose a high-resolution camera or smartphone camera. This will enable you to highlight the specifics of your goods and increase its allure to potential customers.

To ensure that your images are steady and devoid of blur, use a tripod or other stabilizing tool when taking them. A polished, expert-looking photo will result from doing this.

The rule of thirds, which stipulates that the subject of the shot should be placed off-center to create a more dynamic and engaging composition, should be taken into account when constructing your photos.

In order to give your shop a unified look and feel, it's crucial to use the same background and setup for all of your product images.

To improve your photographs and make them more visually appealing, you can also use editing options like brightness, contrast, cropping, and filters.

The chances of generating a sale will increase if you take numerous images of your products from various perspectives so that clients can see the thing in depth.

Understanding the basics of photo editing and how to use tools like Lightroom and Photoshop

Your product images can be improved and made more aesthetically pleasing for potential customers with the appropriate editing methods and tools. Here are some pointers for learning the fundamentals of photo editing and using applications like Lightroom and Photoshop:

Two of the most used picture editing software packages are Lightroom and Photoshop. Lightroom is used mostly for non-destructive editing, such as changing exposure, color, and contrast, whereas Photoshop is used primarily for more complex editing, such as eliminating blemishes and defects, as well as adding text and graphics.

When editing your images, it's crucial to keep the composition in mind and make changes that improve the picture's overall style. The brightness, contrast, cropping, and removal of any blemishes or faults can all be part of this process.

To make sure that the colors in your photo are accurate and consistent, color grading and correction should also be used. A polished, professional-looking shot may result from doing this.

You may use the sliders in Lightroom to change the exposure, contrast, highlights, shadows, whites, and blacks. You can also change the colors by adjusting the sliders for color temperature, tint, and vibrance.

You can eliminate any undesirable components or flaws in Photoshop by using the Clone Stamp tool and any faults can be eliminated by using the Healing Brush tool. The text and shape tools can also be used to add graphics and text to your photos.

Additionally, filters and presets can be used to instantly improve your images and give them a certain mood or aesthetic.

You can create polished and expert-looking product photos that will improve your chances of closing a deal by adjusting the overall composition, brightness and contrast, cropping, erasing blemishes and imperfections, color grading, using the Clone Stamp and Healing Brush tools, adding graphics and text, and using filters and presets.

Creating attention-grabbing product titles and descriptions that increase click-through rates

The following advice will help you write captivating product titles and descriptions that will enhance click-through rates:

It's crucial to utilize keywords that appropriately describe the product and that customers might type into search engines when coming up with product titles. Your products will be more visible in search results as a result of this.

Additionally, it's crucial to employ buzzwords and phrases like "unique," "handmade," "limited edition," and "on sale" to compel shoppers to click on your products.

Keep product titles succinct and to the point, ideally 5-10 words, and be sure to use keywords and action phrases.

It's crucial to use clear, succinct language that precisely defines the characteristics, measurements, and materials of the product when writing product descriptions.

Additionally, you can emphasize the advantages of the product and create a sense of urgency by using compelling language.

Make the material easy to read by using bullet points, and add a call to action that nudges readers to make a purchase.

You can also add other details like delivery details, maintenance instructions, or any special offers or discounts you might be running.

Techniques for creating a consistent branding across all your product listings

Establishing a consistent color scheme and visual appeal that supports your brand is crucial first. This may entail employing a particular palette of hues, fonts, and design components throughout all of your product listings.

Whether it's a lighthearted and humorous tone or a more sober and professional one, you should also employ identical language and tone throughout all of your product descriptions.

Make sure the lighting, composition, and editing styles are the same across all of your product photographs.

Along with giving a link to your shop in every listing, you should also utilize the same logo and graphics on all of your social media channels and product listings.

Making sure your product descriptions and titles are consistent in terms of language, tone, and style is another crucial component of consistent branding.

To organize your products, you can make use of the same tags, categories, and sections.

Using comparable packaging, labels, and business cards will help you keep your branding consistent throughout all of your product listings.

How to use tags, keywords and categories to increase visibility of your products

You can ensure that customers looking for products comparable to yours may easily locate your products by using these methods. You can utilize tags, keywords, and categories to increase the visibility of your products by following the suggestions below:

It is first necessary to comprehend the differences between tags, keywords, and categories. You can add tags, which are specific terms or phrases, to your product listings to help customers find your products when they perform certain keyword searches. Keywords, which are longer terms, are used to convey the broad notion or theme of your products. Categories are the main sections of Etsy's marketplace where customers can look for products.

It's important to use tags as precisely as you can. Instead of using a general tag like "jewelry," you should use specialized tags like "handmade earrings" or "diamond pendant."

It's also essential to use every one of the 13 tags that Etsy lets you to use for each item. Make use of a range of broad and specific tags, and try to include any potential customer search terms.

It's important to undertake keyword research to determine the search terms consumers use to find products similar to yours. Use tools like Google Trends or Google Keyword Planner to find the most popular terms.

When it comes to categories, it's important to choose the right one for your products. To make it simpler for customers to find your products, select the category that best fits them.

Using keywords in your product titles, descriptions, and tags in addition to tags, keywords, and categories is essential for optimizing your product listings.

Tips for creating a visually appealing shop layout that enhances the customer experience

A well-planned store layout can raise customers' likelihood of making a purchase, make it simpler for them to find the items they're looking for, and ultimately boost revenue. Here are some guidelines for designing a shop layout that is visually appealing and improves the shopping experience:

First and foremost, it's crucial to maintain a tidy and clear retail layout. This means limiting the number of colors, typefaces, and images you use because doing so might make your store look busy and overpowering. Instead, use a straightforward, basic style that will be simple for clients to use to browse your store.

Next, think about where you want to put your merchandise. Customers may find it simpler to find what they want if related products are grouped together and presented in a visually pleasing fashion.

Additionally, it's crucial to use excellent product photos across your shop. Customers will have a clearer understanding of what they are purchasing as a result, which may encourage them to make a purchase.

Including a shop banner that symbolizes your business and provides a uniform look and feel across all of your pages is another crucial component of making a visually appealing shop layout.

A fantastic method to improve the shopping experience for customers is by using sections to categorize your products. It makes it simple for customers to go through your products and find what they need.

You might also think about utilizing a unique shop theme or template in addition to these suggestions. These can help your shop look and feel more polished and professional and can help it stand out from the competition.

Understanding the importance of creating a consistent and professional image across all marketing materials

In order to establish credibility and trust with your customers, it is essential to project a consistent and professional image throughout all of your marketing materials. It aids in building your brand and communicating the worth of your items, which may ultimately result in higher sales. Here are some pointers for presenting a unified and expert image in all of your marketing materials:

Establishing a consistent brand identity should come first. Creating a logo, color scheme, and typography that define your brand and can be applied to all of your marketing materials is part of this process.

The usage of top-notch visuals and imagery in all of your marketing materials is also crucial. Images of your products as well as graphics for your store banner, social media, and other marketing materials are included in this.

Additionally, make certain that all of your assets are flawless, polished, and error-free. This calls for careful attention to the finer points of syntax and spelling as well as thoughtful consideration for the layout and readability of your products.

Consistent messaging should be used in all of your marketing materials. To do this, use consistent language and tone while emphasizing the same main points and advantages of your items.

Optimizing your information for numerous platforms is a crucial part of presenting a consistent and expert picture. This entails making certain that your documents are device-optimized and simple to read and navigate across a variety of screens.

In addition to following these suggestions, you should routinely evaluate and update your documents to make sure they remain current and pertinent. This will make sure that your materials continue to persuade buyers of the worth of your goods and foster their faith.

In order to establish credibility and trust with your customers, it is essential to project a consistent and professional image throughout all of your marketing materials. You can successfully communicate the value of your products, establish your brand, and ultimately boost your sales by creating a consistent brand identity, utilizing high-quality images and graphics, making sure that your materials are polished and professional, using consistent messaging, optimizing your materials for various platforms, and routinely reviewing and updating your materials.

How to use lifestyle photos to showcase your products in context and increase desirability.

To make your products more desirable and to boost sales, use lifestyle images to show them off in use. Lifestyle shots show your products being used by actual people in actual scenarios and in a natural environment. Customers can better grasp how to use and incorporate your products into their own life with the help of this style of photography.

Here are some pointers for showcasing your items and making them more desirable by using lifestyle photos:

To start, it's crucial to pick the ideal location for your lifestyle photography. Depending on the kind of goods you're selling, this could be a house, workplace, or outdoor setting. The location need to be visually pleasing and pertinent to your intended audience.

The next step is to use models in the lifestyle shots to highlight your merchandise. The models should be relatable, representative of your target market, and demonstrate genuine and natural usage of your items.

When taking lifestyle shots, it's crucial to pay attention to lighting, composition, and styling. The pictures should have good lighting and be put together in a way that draws attention to the goods. The styling need to reflect your brand and speak to your intended audience.

Utilizing lifestyle photography also means showcasing your goods in a variety of contexts and situations. This might make your items more appealing to clients by assisting them in visualizing how they might use them in their own lives.

In addition to these suggestions, you may make your products more appealing by including lifestyle images on your website, social media accounts, and other marketing collateral. Customers will gain a better understanding of how to use and incorporate your products into their own lives as a result of this.

5

MARKETING AND PROMOTION

Utilizing social media to promote your shop and products

The best approach to raise brand awareness and boost sales is through promoting your store and items on social media. Social media platforms include a variety of tools and features that can assist you in reaching and interacting with your target audience as well as cost-effectively promoting your goods. Here are some pointers for promoting your store and items on social media:

Establishing a presence on the social media channels that are most pertinent to your company comes first. Depending on your target market and the kind of things you're selling, this may include websites like Facebook, Instagram, Twitter, Pinterest, and others.

The next step is to make a content calendar that specifies the kind of material you'll publish on social media platforms and when. This can assist you in maintaining organization and ensuring that you regularly share worthwhile, pertinent, and interesting information with your fans.

Using social media to develop relationships with your current and potential consumers is another crucial component of doing so. This entails connecting with your followers in a way that promotes trust and loyalty and promptly and professionally responding to comments, messages, and reviews.

It's crucial to promote your items on social media in a way that is consistent with your brand and messaging. This entails posting links to your products along with high-quality photos and videos in your social media posts.

Social media should be used to promote your website and store. This can be accomplished by putting connections to your store or website in your bio and posts, as well as by running social media advertisements that cater to particular demographics.

In addition to these recommendations, you may use social media to hold sales-boosting promos, giveaways, and competitions.

You can effectively reach and engage with your target audience and promote your products in a cost-effective manner by establishing a presence on the most pertinent social media platforms, creating a content calendar, creating relationships with customers and potential customers, promoting your products in a way that is consistent with your brand, driving traffic to your website and shop, and running promotions, giveaways, and contests.

Building a following and engaging with customers

You may boost customer happiness, drive sales, and brand awareness by interacting with your audience and developing a devoted following. Here are some pointers for growing your audience and interacting with buyers on Etsy:

First and foremost, it's crucial to constantly offer first-rate client service. This entails promptly and professionally responding to client questions, resolving any problems or concerns that may occur, and going above and beyond to make sure that your customers are satisfied.

The next step is to connect with your audience on social media and other internet channels in order to grow your business. This could involve providing updates about your store, your items, and your brand on websites like Facebook, Instagram, Twitter, Pinterest, and others.

Using email marketing to stay in touch with your consumers is a crucial part of growing a following and engaging with customers. This entails distributing consistent newsletters, advertisements, and other communications that will help you stay in touch with your clients and maintain their interest in your company.

Utilizing consumer feedback and reviews to enhance your offerings and operations is also crucial. This entails regularly monitoring customer reviews, replying to them, and utilising their comments to alter and enhance your offerings and operations.

In order to promote your products and business, you should also use client reviews and success stories. This can assist you in establishing credibility and trust with your clients and in promoting your company in a favorable and genuine manner.

In addition to these suggestions, you can connect with your clients and develop a following by participating in events, pop-up shops, and other offline activities.

Using paid advertising and influencer marketing to increase visibility

Increasing visibility and boosting sales for your Etsy business can be accomplished by using paid advertising and influencer marketing. While influencer marketing enables you to use other well-known accounts' reach and influence to promote your items, paid advertising enables you to target particular audiences. Here are some pointers for leveraging influencer marketing and paid advertising to make your Etsy shop more visible:

Finding the platforms and channels that are most appropriate for your company comes first. Depending on your target market and the kind of things you're selling, this may include websites like Facebook, Instagram, Pinterest, Google, and others.

The next step is to clearly define the objectives and goals of your sponsored advertising initiatives. This can entail boosting website traffic, boosting sales, or raising brand recognition.

Using data and analytics to monitor and evaluate the effectiveness of your campaigns is another crucial component of paid advertising. This entails periodically evaluating the data and modifying your campaigns to maximize their effectiveness.

Utilizing influencer marketing is crucial if you want to reach new audiences and make your items more visible. This entails locating influencers in your niche who have a sizable and active audience and collaborating with them to produce sponsored content or projects that advertise your goods.

To increase traffic to your website and store, you ought to use influencer marketing and paid advertising as well. You can accomplish this by incorporating links to your store or website in your sponsored content and advertisements.

In addition to these suggestions, you may run promotions, giveaways, and competitions that can raise awareness and boost sales by using paid advertising and influencer marketing.

Understanding the importance of marketing and promotion for driving sales on Etsy

Here are some pointers for comprehending how crucial marketing and advertising are to increasing sales on Etsy:

First, it's critical to recognize the relationship between marketing and promotion. Promotion is the precise technique utilized to carry out marketing, which is the general plan for advertising your goods and brand.

To reach your target demographic, you should then employ a number of marketing and advertising strategies. This might involve paid advertising, content marketing, influencer marketing, social media marketing, email marketing, and more.

Utilizing data and analytics to monitor and evaluate the success of your efforts is another crucial component of marketing and promotion. This entails periodically evaluating the data and modifying your campaigns to maximize their effectiveness.

Additionally, it's critical to leverage content and storytelling to engage your audience on an emotional level and effectively market your goods.

In order to quickly communicate your brand's message and catch attention, you need also use images.

In addition to these suggestions, you may employ marketing and promotion to hold sales-boosting promos, giveaways, and competitions.

Tips for creating a social media strategy that aligns with your brand and niche

Social networking sites like Instagram, Facebook, Pinterest, and TikTok provide you the chance to interact with potential clients and aesthetically enticingly present your goods. The following advice will help you develop a social media plan that fits your brand and niche:

Finding the platforms and channels that are most appropriate for your company comes first. Your target market and the kind of goods you're offering will determine this. For instance, Instagram and Pinterest may be more appropriate than TikTok if you sell handmade jewelry.

The next step is to clearly define the objectives and goals of your social media strategy. This can entail boosting website traffic, boosting sales, or raising brand recognition.

Utilizing data and analytics to monitor and evaluate the success of your efforts is another crucial component of a successful social media strategy. This entails frequently analyzing the data and modifying your social media initiatives to enhance their effectiveness.

Additionally, it's critical to leverage content and storytelling to engage your audience on an emotional level and effectively market your goods.

In order to quickly communicate your brand's message and catch attention, you need also use images.

Along with following these pointers, you should engage with your clients on social media by swiftly responding to their queries and resolving any issues they may have. Customers' trust and loyalty can be increased as a result.

Additionally, you ought to leverage your social media accounts to host sales-boosting events like giveaways and competitions.

Best practices for building a following and engaging with customers on platforms like Instagram and Facebook

Social media networks give you the chance to interact with potential clients and aesthetically enticingly present your goods. The following are some effective practices for growing an audience and interacting with clients on websites like Instagram and Facebook:

First and foremost, it's crucial to post frequently and consistently. This entails planning your material ahead of time and maintaining a posting schedule. This will keep your followers interested in your products and engaged.

The next step is to employ pertinent hashtags and keywords to make your postings more visible. Potential clients will locate your products more easily as a result.

Making an emotional connection with your audience and compellingly showcasing your items are two additional crucial components of growing a following and interacting with clients.

In order to quickly communicate your brand's message and catch attention, you need also use images.

Along with following these pointers, you should engage with your clients on social media by swiftly responding to their queries and resolving any issues they may have. Customers' trust and loyalty can be increased as a result.

Additionally, you ought to leverage your social media accounts to host sales-boosting events like giveaways and competitions.

In order to boost engagement and create a feeling of community among your followers, it's also crucial to employ Instagram and Facebook technologies like Instagram stories, IGTV, live videos, Facebook live, and Facebook groups.

You may enhance visibility, drive sales, and cultivate consumer trust and loyalty by publishing frequently, utilizing pertinent hashtags, employing storytelling and images, engaging with your audience, running promotions, and using Instagram and Facebook features.

Techniques for using paid advertising, such as Facebook ads and Instagram sponsored posts, to increase visibility and drive traffic to your shop

Paid promotion, like Facebook advertisements and Instagram sponsored posts, can be an effective technique for raising awareness of and attracting customers to your Etsy store. These advertising methods can help you reach a broader audience and improve your chances of closing a deal when used properly. Here are some methods for using paid advertising to promote your business and attract customers:

Setting specific goals for your advertising strategy is crucial first. This could entail raising brand recognition, attracting customers to your store, or generating a certain volume of sales.

The next step is to conduct research on your target market and develop a buyer persona. You will gain a better understanding of the characteristics, pursuits, and conduct of your ideal client as a result.

Making aesthetically beautiful and captivating advertisements that capture attention and effectively convey your brand's message is another crucial component of employing paid advertising.

A/B testing should be used to improve your adverts and identify the most effective ad styles and wording.

To make sure that your advertising are being seen by the proper people, you should use targeting choices like geography, age, gender, interests, and behaviors when generating your ads.

Additionally, you should regularly monitor the effectiveness of your campaign and change as necessary in light of the data.

Utilizing retargeting and remarketing when using paid advertising is another crucial component. You may increase your chances of making a sale by retargeting and remarketing to clients who have already interacted with your brand.

In addition to these suggestions, you want to think about utilizing Facebook and Instagram's e-commerce services, such as buying on Facebook and Instagram shops, to increase sales.

How to collaborate with influencers and bloggers to promote your products

Working with bloggers and influencers can be an effective approach to market your goods and raise awareness of your Etsy store. Influencer marketing can assist in expanding your audience and raising your chances of closing a deal. Here are some pointers for working with bloggers and influencers to market your products:

Make a list of influencers and bloggers who are compatible with your brand by first researching those in your niche. Find bloggers and influencers who connect well with their audience and have a sizable following.

Next, get in touch with the bloggers and influencers on your list to introduce your company. Tell them about your products and how a partnership would be advantageous for both of you.

It's crucial to be respectful and professional when contacting bloggers and influencers.

Clearly defining the conditions and expectations of the relationship before working with influencers and bloggers is another crucial step. The duration of the partnership, the quantity of posts or mentions, and the payment for their services are a few examples.

The influencer or blogger should also be given a discount code or exclusive offer to share with their audience in order to increase sales.

Monitoring the collaboration's performance and determining its efficacy is also crucial. This may involve keeping tabs on sales, social media activity, and website traffic.

Along with these suggestions, you might think about working with bloggers and influencers to produce user-generated content. User-generated content can support the development of your brand's credibility and trust.

In conclusion, working with bloggers and influencers can be a highly effective approach to market your goods and raise the profile of your Etsy store. You may boost visibility, improve traffic, and boost sales by doing research on bloggers and influencers in your industry, professionally contacting them, establishing clear terms and expectations, making a special offer, monitoring the success of the partnership, and producing user-generated content.

Understanding the importance of email marketing and how to create an email list

Building and expanding an Etsy shop requires using email marketing. You may establish personal connections with your customers using email marketing, which will help you grow your business. The following advice will help you comprehend the significance of email marketing and how to build an email list:

First, it's critical to comprehend the significance of email marketing. You can interact with your customers and develop relationships with them directly through email marketing. You can advertise new products, provide discounts, and let customers know about specials and events.

The next step is to build an email list in order to launch an email marketing campaign. This can be achieved by gathering the email addresses of customers who make purchases from your store or by providing a sign-up incentive to those who do.

It's crucial to check that you have the appropriate consent from your subscribers before building your email list. This indicates that they have freely chosen to receive emails from your store.

To get clients to join your email list, you may use a variety of tools including opt-in forms or lead magnets.

It's crucial to segment your email list once you have one. By using segmentation, you may target particular client groups with relevant content. For instance, you can divide your list into clients who have already made purchases from your store and those who have merely subscribed to your email list.

Making interesting content is a crucial component of email marketing. Your emails should be legible and well-written. Additionally, they have to offer your clients value, like special discounts or access to your company's inner workings.

Monitoring the effectiveness of your email marketing initiatives is also crucial. Metrics like open rates, click-through rates, and conversion rates can be a part of this.

Building and expanding an Etsy shop requires using email marketing. You can interact with your consumers personally, forge bonds, and boost sales by realizing the value of email marketing, building an email list, segmenting it, producing compelling content, and monitoring results.

Tips for creating engaging email campaigns that drive sales

The following advice can help you create email campaigns that will interest your clients and increase sales:

- Personalization: Email marketing relies heavily on personalization. To make the email feel more personalized, use the customer's name in the subject line and throughout the message. Additionally, you can segment your email list to send targeted information to particular customer groups.
- A clear call-to-action: Ensure that the call to action in your emails is crystal clear. Make sure the call-to-action is simple to locate and comprehend whether you want customers to sign up for a special offer, buy a new product, or visit your store.
- Attention-grabbing subject lines: When customers get your email, the subject line is the first thing they will see. Ensure that it is compelling and pertinent to the email's content.
- Engaging and visually appealing content: Your emails should be legible and well-written. Make the emails more entertaining by using pictures, videos, and GIFs. Additionally, make sure that the content offers your customers value, such as special discounts or behind-the-scenes tours of your company.
- Timing is important: When it comes to email marketing, timing is crucial. Sending emails at a moment when your clients are most likely to check their inbox is crucial. You can schedule your emails using tools as well.

- Track and measure the performance: Monitoring the effectiveness of your email marketing initiatives is crucial. Metrics like open rates, click-through rates, and conversion rates can be a part of this. Utilize this information to improve your upcoming promotions and boost sales.

You may improve client engagement and boost sales by personalizing emails, having a clear call to action, coming up with eye-catching subject lines, offering interesting and aesthetically pleasing content, and tracking and measuring performance.

How to use SEO techniques to increase visibility of your shop and products on Etsy search

By using SEO strategies, you may improve the visibility of your store and its products on Etsy searches, which may drive up traffic and boost sales. Here are some pointers for utilizing SEO to improve your presence on Etsy:

- Use keywords in your shop and product listings: The words and phrases people use to search for things on Etsy are known as keywords. Make sure your shop's name, sections, product titles, tags, and descriptions contain pertinent keywords. To find the most effective keywords for your items, use tools like Google's Keyword Planner.
- Optimize your shop sections: Your shop's categories are analogous to its sections. Use keywords in the section names and separate your products into distinct categories to help shoppers locate what they're looking for.
- Use high-quality product photos: An vital component of any Etsy listing are the product images. Make sure your product images are of a high standard, beautifully lit, and appealing to the eye. This will make your products more noticeable in search engine rankings.

- Use tags: Similar to keywords, tags direct shoppers to your products. Use the 13 tags that Etsy provides and relevant keywords to describe your products.
- Optimize your shop announcement and about page: Your shop's announcement and about page functions similarly to the home page. Use keywords and describe your store and what makes you different from the competition in these pages.
- Utilize Etsy's promoted listing feature: You can pay to have your listings appear at the top of search results using Etsy's promoted listings option. This might raise awareness and generate traffic to your store.
- Track your progress: To monitor your progress and assess how your shop is doing, use Etsy's analytics tool. Utilize this information to modify your store and raise your ranking on Etsy searches.

Techniques for analyzing the performance of your marketing and promotion efforts and making data-driven decisions.

You may maximize your efforts and notice a substantial rise in traffic and sales by tracking important indicators and making adjustments in response to the data. The following methods can be used to evaluate the success of your marketing and promotion efforts:

- Use Etsy's analytics tool: With the use of Etsy's analytics tool, you can keep tabs on important statistics like views, favorites, and purchases. Utilize this tool to monitor the effectiveness of your business and individual listings and to spot trends and patterns.
- Monitor your social media metrics: Track important data like engagement, reach, and click-through rates if you're using social media to advertise your store. This will show you in crystal clear detail which postings are succeeding and which ones are failing.

- Track your website and email metrics: Track important data like website traffic, open rates, and conversion rates if you have a website or email list. This will provide you with a clear image of the effectiveness of your website and email efforts.
- Use Google Analytics: Using Google Analytics, you can monitor website traffic, bounce rates, and other crucial indicators. Utilize this tool to learn more about how users interact with your website and to spot any areas that could have improvement.
- Monitor your competitors: Observe your rivals and learn from what they are doing well. You may use the same tactics in your own shop if you know what works for them.
- Use A/B testing: Comparing two iterations of a website or marketing campaign with A/B testing allows you to see which one works better. Use this technique to test several headlines, pictures, and other components to find which ones perform the best.
- Use surveys and customer feedback: To learn what customers like and dislike about your store, use surveys and customer feedback. You will gain useful knowledge from this about how to enhance your store and goods.

6

OPTIMIZING AND MANAGING YOUR SHOP

Understanding and utilizing Etsy's analytics tools

You may use these tools to keep tabs on crucial statistics for your shop and individual listings, such as views, clicks, and sales. You may improve the performance of your shop and obtain insightful information about it by routinely examining this data and making data-driven decisions.

The "Stats" section, which offers a thorough picture of your shop's performance, including views, favorites, and purchases, is one important feature. You can separate this data by time frame and individual postings to find patterns and trends. The "Traffic" area is another crucial feature because it provides you with a breakdown of the sources of your views, including social media, external search engines, and Etsy search.

Additionally, you can monitor how your store performs for different search terms using Etsy's analytics tools, which can help you tweak your listings for higher rankings in search results. You can improve the alignment of your titles and tags with what buyers are searching for by routinely tracking the performance of your shop on particular keywords.

Use third-party analytics tools, such as Facebook Page Insights for your social media presence or Google Analytics for your website, in addition to these built-in ones to monitor your effectiveness across various marketing channels.

Managing inventory and fulfillment

A system for monitoring your inventory levels, processing orders, and shipping goods must be in place.

Monitoring your inventory levels frequently and placing reorders as necessary is a crucial part of inventory management. A spreadsheet or specialist inventory management software can be used for this. In order to keep consumers informed of any delays and to allow you to make necessary plans, it's also critical to have a mechanism in place for tracking and managing backorders.

It's crucial to have a system in place for processing orders as they come in fast and effectively when it comes to fulfillment. Additionally, shipping labels must be created, order confirmations must be sent, and inventory levels must be updated. Additionally, it's critical to have policies in place that are explicit and comprehensive and provide information on projected shipping timeframes as well as any additional costs.

Making sure that the items you are selling are packaged and dispatched in a way that will protect them throughout transportation is another crucial component of fulfillment. This entails using appropriate packaging supplies, including bubble wrap, and legible labeling.

Additionally, it's critical to keep track of any returns or exchanges that might occur and to have a transparent and equitable procedure in place for handling them.

Overall, keeping track of inventory and fulfilling orders can be a time-consuming effort, but by putting a system in place and maintaining organization, you can make sure that the process is quick and easy for both you and your clients. You may boost client happiness, lower the chance of mistakes and refunds, and ultimately boost revenue by offering a frictionless experience.

Optimizing your shop for search and visibility

Customers who conduct a product search on Etsy are shown a list of pertinent results. By optimizing your store, you may raise the likelihood that your products will show up first in search results, which will improve traffic and revenue to your store.

Using pertinent keywords and tags in your product titles, descriptions, and tags is one of the most important aspects of optimizing your shop for search. By using these keywords, Etsy's search algorithm can better match your products with pertinent search queries and comprehend what they are about. It's crucial to pick keywords that are both pertinent to your items and widely used by customers. To find the most relevant terms for your niche, you can use tools like Google Keyword Planner.

Using high-quality photos is a crucial part of optimizing your shop for search. It's crucial to take and edit excellent product photos since customers are more inclined to click on products that have appealing visuals.

It's also critical to frequently introduce fresh merchandise and special offers to your store. This can improve exposure in search results and keep your store looking new and relevant to customers.

Having a neat and appealing shop layout is another crucial component in optimizing your store. In order to achieve a polished and uniform appearance and feel, this includes designing sections to group relevant products and employing high-quality photos and graphics.

In order to boost the visibility of your business, it's crucial to utilize all the tools and capabilities that Etsy offers. These include leveraging promoted listings and Etsy's marketing and advertising tools to draw customers to your store.

Understanding and managing your costs, expenses and taxes

This part will discuss the value of knowing your financial situation and how to keep track of your expenses. We will also go over how to price your goods so that you can make a profit and pay your expenses.

Knowing where your money is going is one of the first stages in managing your expenses. Materials, shipping, and any other costs associated with your business are included in this. It's critical to maintain track of these costs so that you can calculate your cost of goods sold (COGS) precisely and determine product prices that will result in a profit.

Understanding your tax obligations is a crucial part of managing expenditures. Understanding what taxes you must pay and when they are due is crucial if you operate a business and are responsible for paying taxes on your revenue. Keep track of this part of your business because failing to pay taxes on time might result in penalties and fines.

We will also discuss methods for reducing costs and identifying strategies to boost revenues in this part. This can involve negotiating lower pricing with suppliers, eliminating waste and inefficiency, and seeking for methods to expand your company.

You will have a thorough understanding of how to manage your costs, expenses, and taxes by the end of this chapter. You will also have the resources necessary to make well-informed decisions about pricing, expenses, and taxes that will help you boost your profitability and advance your Etsy business.

Overview of the different analytics tools available on Etsy and how to use them to track sales and customer behavior

It's essential for Etsy sellers to comprehend and make use of the platform's analytics features. These technologies can offer insightful data on your sales and consumer behavior, enabling you to optimize your store for success and make data-driven decisions.

The Shop Stats tab on Etsy, which presents an overview of your sales, views, and other crucial indicators, is one of the most significant analytics tools. You can monitor your progress on this page, spot trends and patterns, and make any corrections. The Listing Stats tab, which offers comprehensive details about the views and sales for each of your listings, also allows you to monitor the performance of your business.

The Traffic Sources report, which enables you to see your traffic's sources, including organic search, direct traffic, and referral traffic, is another crucial tool. You can use this information to determine which marketing and promotion strategies are effective and where to concentrate your future efforts.

In-depth data regarding consumer activity is also made available by Etsy, including average order value, return customer rate, and conversion rate. You may use these data to evaluate the overall health of your store and pinpoint its potential for growth.

Tips for managing inventory and ensuring that products are always in stock

This chapter will cover several methods and approaches for controlling inventory and maintaining the efficiency of your store.

The establishment of a system for monitoring stock levels is a crucial component of inventory management. A spreadsheet or specialist inventory management software can be used for this. This will make it simple for you to identify the goods that are selling quickly and those that could require reordering.

Demand projection is a crucial component of inventory management. This can be achieved by reviewing historical sales data and accounting for any impending events or promotions that can have an impact on sales. You can make sure you have enough inventory on hand to satisfy consumer needs by predicting demand.

In addition to controlling stock levels, it's critical to make sure that your products are consistently in good shape. This entails frequently checking products for flaws and keeping them appropriately to prevent damage.

It's critical to have a system in place for processing and dispatching orders quickly when it comes to fulfillment. Printing shipping labels, making packing slips, and keeping track of tracking numbers are some examples of this. You can make sure that purchases are shipped out fast and that consumers are satisfied by optimizing your fulfillment process.

Understanding the prices connected with your products is a crucial component of inventory management. This covers all costs, including the price of the materials and labor as well as packaging, shipping, and any extra charges. Understanding your costs will help you set fair prices for your goods and calculate profit margins.

You may manage your inventory more profitably and efficiently on Etsy by applying these tactics, as well as by keeping track of your expenditures, expenses, and taxes.

How to optimize your shop for search and visibility on Etsy

Making ensuring that your shop and products are readily visible to potential clients is one of the most crucial aspects of developing a successful Etsy business. Search engine optimization (SEO) can help with this. You may improve your shop's exposure on Etsy, get more customers there, and eventually increase sales by employing numerous strategies to optimize your shop and listings for search.

Your shop name and title should be one of the first things you take into account when optimizing your shop for search. Make sure your store's name is distinctive, memorable, and accurately represents your brand and market. Incorporate keywords from phrases that potential clients would use to search for products similar to yours into the title of your store.

The tags and keywords you use in your listings, in addition to your shop name and title, are crucial for SEO. To ensure that your products appear in pertinent search results, include relevant keywords in the names, tags, and descriptions of your products. A range of keywords should be used to cater for the many methods that customers may search for your products.

Your shop's design and branding should be taken into account while optimizing it for search. Ensure that the logo and store banner are representative of your business and the design of your products. Make sure your store is visually appealing and simple to navigate because these features can draw customers in and keep them interested.

Finally, it's critical to periodically check your shop's statistics and make adjustments in light of the information. Several analytics tools are available on Etsy to assist you in monitoring the performance of your shop and making fact-based decisions. Utilize this information to keep tabs on which products are selling well, which search terms are generating the most traffic, and which marketing strategies are producing the highest levels of revenue. You can continue to optimize your shop and listings for search by routinely reviewing and analyzing your metrics, which will ultimately result in greater visibility and increased revenue.

Techniques for tracking expenses and understanding profit margins

To sustain profitability and make wise business decisions, Etsy sellers must have a thorough awareness of their costs, expenses, and taxes. Understanding your profit margins and keeping a frequent tab on your spending are two important methods to achieve this. Making a budget and carefully tracking your income and expenses will help you achieve this.

It's crucial to take into account all facets of your business, such as materials, labor, and transportation, while controlling your expenditures. You may set prices that are reasonable for the client and lucrative for your business by knowing the costs associated with each product. It's also crucial to account for the cost of any tools or equipment you might need to buy in order to manufacture your goods.

Understanding taxes is a crucial part of controlling your expenses. You will be accountable for paying taxes on your income as an Etsy seller, therefore it's critical to understand the local tax regulations. To make sure you are in compliance with all laws and regulations, it is also a good idea to speak with a tax expert.

It's critical to control your inventory in addition to your costs. This entails tracking the products you have on hand as well as predicting demand in the future. You can make sure that your products are constantly available and that you don't overstock or understock by setting up a reliable inventory management system.

Finally, it's crucial to employ pertinent tags and keywords, maintain your shop and products organized, and optimize your shop for search and visibility on Etsy. Adding new merchandise and offering specials on a regular basis can also help your store become more visible and attract more customers. You can use these methods to create data-driven decisions that will enhance the performance of your shop while routinely reviewing your statistics.

Understanding the importance of cash flow management and how to maintain a positive cash flow

A solid grasp of cash flow management is essential for managing a profitable Etsy business. A strong cash flow is crucial to ensuring that your company has the resources it needs to run and expand. Cash flow refers to the movement of money into and out of your firm.

Maintaining a solid cash flow depends heavily on keeping close tabs on your expenses and comprehending your profit margins. You'll have a better notion of where to make expense reductions or revenue increases if you know how much money is coming into and leaving your company, as well as where it is being spent.

Understanding the significance of maintaining appropriate inventory levels is another key component of cash flow management. Cash flow issues can result from overstocking products because you might end up paying for inventory that isn't moving rapidly enough. Understocking, on the other hand, can result in missed sales opportunities.

Additionally, it's crucial to optimize your shop for Etsy search and visibility. Using pertinent keywords and tags in your product listings, making sure that your shop's branding and appearance are expert and consistent, and using analytics tools to monitor your shop's success are all ways to do this.

Finally, it's critical to understand the many taxes and rules that are relevant to your company. You may avoid any potential legal problems and make sure that your company is operating properly by adhering to all pertinent rules and regulations.

Tips for streamlining and automating processes to increase efficiency

Finding ways to automate and streamline operations will help you run a successful Etsy business and enhance productivity. Utilizing equipment and programs that assist with activities like inventory control, order fulfillment, and customer service is one method to achieve this. For instance, by conveniently tracking stock levels, generating invoices and packing slips, and automating shipping labels, utilizing a technology like Shopify to manage your inventory and orders can save a significant amount of time and effort.

Additionally, employing a CRM system may help you stay organized and keep track of customer interactions, which can be particularly useful when it comes to following up with leads and offering top-notch customer care. Using automation tools like bots and macros to carry out repetitive tasks, like sending follow-up emails or updating product listings, is another method for boosting productivity.

Creating a system for handling your money and creating a budget for costs is another crucial component of streamlining and automating activities. This can involve planning a budget for costs like materials, shipping, and marketing as well as regularly monitoring your income and outgoing costs. Understanding and preparing for taxes, such as income and sales taxes, is also crucial. You'll be better prepared to make data-driven decisions and take action to increase your cash flow if you have a comprehensive grasp of your finances.

Understanding the basics of accounting and bookkeeping for an Etsy business

Understanding balance sheets and other financial statements, as well as keeping track of spending and income. You can make smart business decisions and secure the financial success of your Etsy business by having a clear understanding of your financial situation.

Monitoring earnings and expenditures is a crucial part of accounting for an Etsy business. This entails keeping track of all cash flows, including cash received from sales and customer payments as well as cash expended on things like operating costs and the cost of items sold. You may better understand your profit margins and decide how much to charge for products and how much to spend by keeping accurate records of these transactions.

Understanding the various financial statements, such as the income statement, which provides an overview of your company's financial performance over time, and the balance sheet, which offers a snapshot of your company's financial situation at a particular point in time, is another crucial component. Regularly monitoring these statements will enable you to see patterns and make necessary modifications to enhance your financial success.

The fundamentals of taxes and compliance for an Etsy business must also be understood. This entails being aware of the requirements for income and sales taxes as well as keeping up with any amendments to the tax code that can have an impact on your company. You can prevent any potential legal complications in the future by adhering to all tax requirements.

In order to maximize productivity, it's crucial to streamline and automate procedures as much as you can. This goes beyond simply mastering the fundamentals of accounting and bookkeeping. Using accounting software, putting in place automated systems for invoicing and payment, and putting in place inventory control measures are a few examples of what is possible. You may focus on expanding your business by doing this, which will save you time and resources.

How to create a budget and financial plan

An essential step in controlling the financial success of your Etsy business is developing a budget and financial plan. It enables you to define financial objectives, keep tabs on expenditures, and make wise resource allocation choices.

It's critical to establish a budget by listing all of your fixed and variable expenses. Rent or mortgage payments are examples of fixed expenses, but the cost of materials is an example of a variable expense that might alter from month to month. You can create financial objectives for your business and figure out how much money you need to make each month to pay your expenses and generate a profit if you have a firm idea of your costs.

The next stage is to put together a financial plan that details the steps you'll take to reach your financial objectives. This can entail raising your prices, broadening your product offering, or developing new promotional strategies for your company. As your business expands and develops, it's crucial to frequently assess and modify your budget and financial strategy.

It's critical to maintain organization and maintain correct financial records in addition to developing a budget and financial strategy. This entails keeping track of all earnings and outlays as well as invoices and receipts for all purchases made for the benefit of the company. This will make it simpler for you to manage your money, submit your taxes, and make financial decisions for your company.

Understanding and complying with tax laws as an Etsy seller

The first step is to apply for a sales tax permit and register for sales tax in the state or states where you will be conducting business. You can collect and send sales tax from your transactions on Etsy by doing this. Use tax registration could be required in some states. Similar to sales tax, use tax is paid by the buyer as opposed to the seller.

The next step is to carefully record and keep track of all of your income and expenses. In order to do this, complete records must be kept of all business dealings, expenditures, and payments made to suppliers and contractors. You could be able to deduct a portion of your utility bills, property taxes, and mortgage interest if you operate a business out of your home.

When it comes to taxes, it's critical to understand any tax credits or deductions for which you may be eligible as an Etsy seller. For instance, the IRS allows for the deductibility of business-related costs such as marketing, office supply, and home office expenses.

It is also essential to consult a tax professional to ensure you are abiding by all state and federal laws and regulations. They can also help you create a budget and financial plan to make sure you are using your resources as efficiently as possible.

Tips for handling and shipping orders and dealing with returns and refunds.

A clear and effective procedure must be in place for handling orders as an Etsy seller, from the time they are received until they are dispatched to the client.

In order to quickly and efficiently fulfill orders and avoid over-selling, it is crucial to maintain accurate and up-to-date inventory records. This will include advice on using software and tools for inventory management to speed up the procedure.

The many shipping choices available to Etsy sellers will next be discussed, including the usage of shipping carriers, shipping labels, and shipping costs. Additionally, we will offer advice on how to properly package and transport products so they arrive in top shape.

Dealing with returns and refunds is one of the most crucial facets of running an online store. We will offer advice on how to manage these circumstances professionally and in a way that is favorable to the consumer, including how to address client complaints and disputes.

Additionally, we'll discuss how to use shipping companies, create mailing labels and shipping quotes, package and send your things effectively, and manage returns and refunds. You will have a thorough understanding of how to manage orders and shipping on Etsy by the end of this chapter, and you'll be able to put best practices into effect to make sure your customers have a successful and easy experience.

7

SCALING YOUR BUSINESS

Strategies for expanding your product line and increasing sales

Adding new product categories or iterations of current products to your lineup is one way to diversify your offerings. For instance, if you already sell handmade jewelry, you can think about expanding your product range to include scarves or handbags.

Utilizing data and client input is another tactic for finding new product ideas. You can determine which products are currently performing well and which products may be underperforming by looking at your shop's stats. You can use this information to help you decide which items to keep making, which to stop making, and which new products to create.

You can also find new product prospects by keeping an eye on trends in your industry or specialty and being open to trying new things.

It's also crucial to keep in mind that growing your product line doesn't always include introducing brand-new products. Expanding the channels via which clients may buy and use your items can be important at times. To boost the value for clients, you might, for instance, think about offering a subscription service or bundle package if you sell digital products.

Additionally, keep in mind that it's essential to maintain the quality of your items and make sure they complement your brand identity as you grow your product range. By doing this, you'll be able to gain the trust and loyalty of your clients, which will ultimately result in higher sales and company expansion for your Etsy shop.

Outsourcing and automating processes for efficiency

You can free up significant time by outsourcing specific duties, such product photography or shipping and packaging, so that you can concentrate on other crucial facets of your company.

Utilizing a fulfillment firm to take care of the storage, packaging, and shipping of your products is one approach to outsource. This might be especially useful if you receive a lot of orders or if you sell bulky or challenging-to-ship items. To manage customer service and administrative work, another option is to hire a virtual assistant.

Efficiency can be greatly improved through automation. You can automate repetitive operations and make it simpler to keep track of critical information with the use of tools like automated email responders, inventory management software, and accounting software. You may integrate numerous apps and automate processes with platforms like IFTTT or Zapier to improve the efficiency of your workflows.

Tips for managing and motivating a team

It can be challenging to lead and inspire a team, but with the appropriate tactics, it is possible to do so successfully.

Prior to anything else, it's critical to specify each team member's tasks and responsibilities. Job descriptions and having clear objectives for each person can help with this. Team members will be better able to comprehend what is expected of them and work toward reaching those expectations if expectations and rules are made explicit.

Next, it's important to communicate clearly. Meetings on a regular basis, whether in person or virtually, can serve to keep everyone in the loop and handle any concerns that might come up. Additionally, giving team members regular constructive and positive feedback will help them realize how they are doing and what they can change to better.

It's also crucial to foster a supportive and upbeat work environment. Regular team-building exercises, encouraging an environment of open communication, and praising and rewarding hard work are all effective ways to achieve this. Team members will be more motivated to achieve and more willing to go above and beyond to support the company's success if a pleasant environment is fostered.

A team might be motivated via incentives and bonuses as well. Recognizing and rewarding hard work may keep team members motivated and involved, whether it's a monetary bonus or a fun team-building exercise.

Finally, it's critical to be flexible and open to changing course when necessary. A more effective and productive team can be built by frequently assessing the team's performance and making modifications. Making adjustments can help to keep the team motivated and moving in the right direction, whether it's through the reorganization of responsibilities, the addition of new team members, or the adoption of new procedures.

Understanding the importance of scaling your business and how to prepare for it

Expanding your product offering, entering new markets, or even recruiting a team to assist in managing your business's operations are all examples of scaling your enterprise. But it's crucial to have a planned approach to scaling and to be ready for the adjustments that occur with expansion.

Understanding your target market and spotting fresh prospects for expansion are two crucial components of scaling. This could entail looking into fresh market niches or product trends, as well as investigating fresh customer-facing channels. To enter a new market, you might opt to build a brick-and-mortar store or sell your products on other e-commerce platforms, for instance, or you might decide to extend your product range to include new things that are consistent with your brand and niche.

Efficiency is a key component in scaling. It's crucial to look for ways to automate and streamline procedures as your company expands if you want to preserve profitability and keep costs in check. Depending on the work at hand, this may entail employing tools and software to automate and manage activities like inventory and order fulfillment or outsourcing some operations, such product photography or customer support.

Scaling your firm involves many different factors, including leading and inspiring a staff. As your business grows, you might need to engage more staff members or freelancers to assist with activities like marketing, product development, and customer service. It's critical to set defined roles and duties, foster a healthy work atmosphere, and offer your team members regular training and assistance.

The financial and legal ramifications of increasing your business must also be considered. This can entail creating a budget and financial plan, comprehending and abiding by tax regulations, and getting expert counsel from an accountant or lawyer.

Tips for expanding your product line and increasing sales through product diversification

It's critical for Etsy vendors to continually consider how to expand and vary their product offerings in order to boost sales and attract new clients. The variety of products is one method for attaining this.

The process of adding new and distinct products to your store in addition to the ones you already have on hand is known as product diversification. By keeping your shop interesting and fresh, this can help you draw in new consumers and keep your current ones.

It's critical to maintain your brand and market niche in mind when thinking about expanding your product line. Look for products that fit your target market and are complementary to the ones you already sell. If you presently sell handcrafted jewelry, for instance, think about expanding into additional accessories like scarves or handbags.

Adding additional iterations or sizes of your present products is another approach to vary your product range. If you sell handcrafted soap, for instance, think about adding other scents or developing a line of travel-sized soaps.

Your efforts at product diversity can also be informed by researching popular products and determining customer wants. To find out what products are in demand and to learn more about what customers want, you can use resources like Google Trends or Etsy's own search statistics.

Additionally, it's critical to consider the costs associated with finding and developing new items, as well as making sure that they will be lucrative. Create a plan for how you will source and produce new product opportunities after you have found them, and consider the possible return on investment.

It's also important to remember that expanding your product line doesn't mean you should stop marketing your current items. Finding ways to enhance and grow what you already have is more important than trying to replace it.

Techniques for outsourcing and automating processes to increase efficiency and reduce workload

This can be accomplished, for example, by outsourcing and automating some procedures. You may free up your time and concentrate on other crucial facets of your business, such as product development and marketing, by outsourcing duties like product photography, graphic design, and customer care. Processes can be streamlined and time saved by using automation solutions like order fulfillment apps and inventory management software.

Finding dependable and trustworthy freelancers or contractors that are familiar with your brand and capable of producing excellent work is crucial when outsourcing. Prospective hires should be thoroughly vetted, and references and samples of their prior work should be requested. Make sure to be specific about your expectations and timeframes for the work.

There are several solutions available to assist you streamline your business when it comes to automation. For instance, order fulfillment apps can handle the delivery procedure for you, while inventory management software can track your stock levels automatically and reorder when necessary. Additionally, there are software like Quick-Books and Xero that can assist with bookkeeping and accounting.

Strategies for managing and motivating a team as your business grows

Setting clear objectives and open lines of communication, as well as offering frequent feedback and chances for advancement, are imperative as you hire more staff members or independent contractors.

Clearly defining each member's tasks and responsibilities is a good team management technique. This makes sure that everyone is aware of what is required of them and can concentrate on their individual tasks. To monitor progress and spot opportunities for growth, it's also crucial to define goals and conduct regular performance reviews.

Additionally, maintaining team members' motivation requires creating a positive and cooperative work atmosphere. Encourage open communication, honor and reward excellence, and offer chances for professional growth.

Giving a team the tools and resources they need to execute their jobs well is a crucial part of team management. This covers stuff like tools, supplies, and software. Additionally, give them support and instruction to help them develop their abilities.

It could also become required as your firm expands to hire other workers or service providers to do specific jobs or responsibilities. Accounting, marketing, and product fulfillment are a few examples of this. When outsourcing, it's crucial to thoroughly investigate potential partners and express your expectations and needs in detail.

Being ready for potential difficulties and obstacles is essential while scaling your firm. It's crucial to be prepared for unforeseen problems, to be adaptive, and to be open to new chances.

Understanding the importance of customer service and how to scale it

Keep in mind that the customer experience should always be your primary concern as your company expands. This entails not only offering first-rate customer service but also scaling it to accommodate an expanding clientele.

Having a thorough and lucid set of customer service policies in place is a crucial component of increasing customer service. These guidelines should address every aspect of your business, including how customers can contact you, the kinds of questions you will answer, and how you manage returns and refunds. In addition to making it simpler for you to respond to customer inquiries, having these policies in place will give your clients a feeling of transparency and trust.

Having a dedicated customer service staff in place is a crucial component of increasing customer service. It might be challenging to manage client inquiries on your own when your firm expands. You may guarantee that all customer concerns are responded to quickly and competently by assembling a team of committed customer service experts.

This crew should be well-versed in your customer service guidelines and equipped to deal with any kind of client enquiry. In order to make sure that all customer concerns are answered promptly, it's also critical to have a system in place for managing and tracking customer enquiries.

Scaling your customer support activities can also be accomplished by making an investment in customer relationship management (CRM) software. These solutions can assist you in managing customer data in one place, automating responses, and tracking client interactions.

Additionally, it's crucial to answer client complaints and issues promptly. You can help avoid negative reviews and keep a good reputation by routinely monitoring customer feedback and taking action to fix any concerns that develop.

In conclusion, expanding customer service is a crucial part of expanding your Etsy business. You can make sure that your clients continue to receive the high-quality service they expect and deserve even as your business grows by having clear policies, a committed workforce, and efficient tools in place.

Tips for creating a business plan and forecasting for growth

Scaling your Etsy business requires you to write a business strategy and project growth. A business plan is a written document that describes the objectives, plans, and financial forecasts of your company. It acts as a road plan for your company and can be used to get finance or track development.

Starting with the identification of your target market and a knowledge of their demands is crucial when writing a business plan. This will assist you in deciding on the goods and services you will provide as well as the methods you will employ to connect with and interact with your target market.

The next step is to create specific, attainable goals for your company. These objectives must to be precise, deadline-driven, and consistent with your entire corporate vision. A few objectives for an Etsy shop might be to increase sales by 20% in the following six months or to amass 1,000 Instagram followers in the following year.

You may create tactics to achieve your goals once you've determined what they are. These tactics ought to be in line with your target audience and ought to consider any potential difficulties or difficulties you might encounter.

It's crucial to be reasonable and cautious while making your financial estimates. This entails taking into consideration variables including overhead charges, marketing costs, and anticipated sales. Additionally, you should take into account the existing business climate as well as any anticipated market trends.

Finally, as your firm develops, it's critical to periodically evaluate and update your business plan. This will assist you in maintaining your course and implementing any necessary corrections as you proceed.

How to create a system for delegating tasks and managing a team

Creating a framework for managing a team and assigning tasks is essential. This will enable you to concentrate on the most crucial elements of your organization, such product development and marketing, in addition to increasing productivity and reducing your workload.

Finding the important tasks that must be completed on a regular basis is one of the first steps in developing a strategy for managing a team. These could involve carrying out orders, making listings, and answering client questions. You can start distributing the work to different team members based on their skills and talents once you have a clear picture of what needs to be done.

Establishing clear communication lines is a crucial part of managing a team. Tools like email, instant messaging, and project management software can be used for this. The staff will be able to stay updated about what's going on in the company and be better prepared to manage any problems that may develop if there are open channels of communication.

It's also crucial to ensure that your team has the resources and training it needs in order for them to be motivated and productive. This can entail giving them access to the necessary software and tools or instructing them on how to complete particular jobs. It's crucial to set up your team members with clear objectives and goals, as well as to give them regular feedback on how they're doing.

It's crucial to periodically assess and modify your team management system as your organization expands. In order to increase productivity, this can entail altering the duties and responsibilities of certain team members or implementing new tools and technology.

Understanding the importance of setting clear goals and expectations for your team

As your Etsy business expands, so will the range of duties and obligations that must be handled. It's crucial to realize that as your company expands, you won't be able to handle everything yourself. You'll need to start assembling a team to assist you in managing and scaling your company. The establishing of clear expectations and goals is one of the most crucial elements of managing a team.

Make sure your team's goals are relevant, time-bound, specific, quantifiable, reachable, and relevant when you set them. The basis for SMART goals is this. Your team will be better able to grasp what needs to be done and how they can support the expansion of your company if you set clear and defined goals. It's crucial to consistently discuss these objectives and to give updates on development.

It's crucial to establish clear expectations for your team in addition to creating goals. Expectations for performance, work ethic, and communication are included. Establishing clear expectations will make it easier to make sure that everyone is on the same page and pursuing the same objectives. Along with giving regular feedback, it's critical to honor team members for their efforts and successes.

Another crucial aspect of managing a team is developing a framework for task delegation. This involves determining each team member's strengths and allocating responsibilities accordingly. It's crucial to express expectations regarding timelines and deliverables as well as to give precise directions. Regular check-ins and progress updates will make sure that everything is moving forward as planned and that any problems can be resolved right away.

Finally, it's crucial to keep in mind that a crucial component of every business, including those operating on Etsy, is customer service. Systems and procedures must be in place as your company expands to guarantee that clients continue to receive top-notch service. This entails promptly responding to consumer concerns, managing returns and refunds effectively, and being proactive in resolving any potential problems.

Tips for creating an effective communication system with your team

Everyone is on the same page and pursuing the same objectives when there is open and regular communication. Here are some pointers for developing a productive team communication system:

Establish regular meetings: Whether they are daily, weekly, or monthly, schedule regular meetings with your staff. Everyone has the chance to provide updates, ask questions, and discuss any problems that may have come up at these meetings.

Use the appropriate communication tools: Email, messaging applications, and project management software are just a few examples of the many communication tools accessible. Make sure everyone is trained on how to use the tools you decide are ideal for your team.

Encourage open communication by cultivating an environment where team members feel free to express their ideas. Encourage honest dialogue, and pay attention to criticism.

Clarify your expectations: Clearly state the duties and expectations of each team member. This will make sure that everyone is aware of their responsibilities and how they contribute to the team's overarching objective.

Ensure that all communications are made in a clear and consistent manner. Avoid using technical or jargon terminology that could confuse some team members.

Follow-up and follow-through: Ensure that you take action on any choices or action items that were agreed upon during meetings. This will guarantee that duties are finished promptly and that everyone is held responsible.

You may establish a productive communication system within your team that will contribute to the success of your company by putting these suggestions into practice. To keep your staff focused, inspired, and engaged, communication must be clear and constant.

How to create a system for measuring and tracking performance for your team.

A crucial component of leading and inspiring a team is developing a system for tracking and measuring performance. This system should be created to offer each team member with specific, quantifiable goals and a mechanism to monitor their progress toward those goals.

Setting up key performance indicators (KPIs) for each team member is one approach to do this. These must to be precise, quantifiable, and consistent with your overarching corporate objectives. If one of your objectives is to grow sales, for instance, a KPI for your sales staff might be the amount of sales generated each month.

A performance tracking system's regular feedback to team members is another crucial component. This should be utilized as a coaching and growth tool, and it should be both constructive and positive. Meeting with team members one-on-one on a regular basis can be a good approach to discuss goals and give feedback.

It's crucial to set up a mechanism for monitoring development and outcomes. Regular reports and data analysis to pinpoint problem areas and track advancement toward objectives could be a part of this. Team members can better understand their contribution to accomplishing the broader goals of the company by having clear and transparent measures for success.

It's crucial to explain the system to your team, make sure everyone is on board, and make sure they all understand their roles and duties in order to successfully measure performance. This entails establishing precise standards and objectives, offering ongoing coaching and feedback, and fostering an atmosphere that promotes candid dialogue and teamwork.

Last but not least, it's critical to keep in mind that the system should be adaptive to the needs of the team and the business. The performance tracking system should expand and change with the company as well in order to maintain its usefulness and efficacy.

8

DEALING WITH CHALLENGES AND OBSTACLES

How to handle negative reviews and customer complaints

Running a business, particularly an Etsy shop, inevitably involves handling bad reviews and consumer complaints. Negative feedback can be challenging to handle, but it's crucial to tackle these circumstances with professionalism and a cool mind. Here are some guidelines for dealing with unfavorable comments and client complaints:

React quickly. The more time a consumer has to reflect on a bad experience, the longer you delay to address a bad review or complaint. A prompt response demonstrates to the client that you are concerned about their experience and are making an effort to allay their worries.

Express regret and accept accountability. Although it may be tempting to defend yourself or lay the blame at someone else's door, it is crucial to accept responsibility for the unhappy customer. An authentic apology can go a long way toward calming uncomfortable circumstances.

Provide a resolution. Offer a solution to the issue once you have acknowledged the client's concerns and apologized. This can be a reimbursement, a substitution item, or a discount ticket for further purchases.

Following up Follow up with the consumer to make sure their

problem has been satisfactorily fixed once you have supplied a solution.

Gain knowledge from the encounter. Consider the customer's complaint carefully and consider what you can change to avoid repeating the same mistakes. Use this criticism to enhance your company's operations and client relations.

Keep it businesslike. Keep in mind that you are representing your brand and that your Etsy shop is a business. Be professional in your comments and refrain from being aggressive or combative.

You may respond to negative feedback and customer complaints in a way that not only answers the client's problems but also enhances your business and customer service by using the advice in this article. Keep in mind that a bad experience can also be a chance to win over a customer to your brand and win them over for good.

Strategies for dealing with competition and saturation in your niche

One strategy for standing out in a crowded market is to concentrate on developing a distinctive brand and providing superior, distinctive items. This can be accomplished by carrying out market research to comprehend client demands, find lucrative niches, design and source items that meet those needs, and uncover profitable niches.

Another tactic is to set yourself apart by providing great customer service. Building trust and loyalty with your consumers can be achieved by responding to their questions and concerns in a timely manner and with professionalism.

Focusing on developing a strong social media presence and using paid advertising and influencer marketing to boost awareness are other ways to stand out in a crowded industry.

Additionally, it's critical to be abreast of the most recent trends and advancements in your specialized field and to be open to experimenting with novel marketing and promotion techniques.

Another tactic is to identify ways to set oneself apart from rival businesses, such as by delivering distinctive goods or services or giving clients an exceptional experience.

It's also critical to be mindful of pricing competition and to make sure that your rates are reasonable while still leaving enough for a profit margin.

Last but not least, it's critical to keep in mind that competition and saturation can be viewed as opportunities rather than threats. You can stay ahead of the curve and continue to expand your business by keeping an eye on what your rivals are doing and always enhancing your own products.

Managing and overcoming burnout and stress

The ongoing need to develop new products, market your store, and meet customer demand can be demanding and can overwhelm a business owner. It's critical to keep in mind that burnout can have a bad impact on both your business and your well-being.

Establishing clear boundaries for oneself is one strategy for managing burnout. This include establishing set working hours and taking time off as necessary. Additionally, it's critical to look after your physical and emotional wellbeing by getting adequate rest, exercising, and engaging in self-care.

Prioritizing and organizing your tasks is a further strategy for stress management. Make a to-do list and rank the most crucial chores according to importance. It's also beneficial to divide more difficult activities into smaller, easier-to-manage components. You can lessen the sense of overwhelm by concentrating on one task at a time.

It's crucial to assign responsibilities to others whenever possible. It becomes impractical to manage everything alone as your company expands. By giving duties to a team, you can concentrate on the aspects of the business where you thrive while having confidence that the other activities are being completed effectively.

A solid support system should be in place as well. Having someone to talk to about the difficulties of operating a business, whether it be a mentor, friend, or therapist, can help you to manage stress and burnout.

Finally, it's critical to keep in mind that taking a break is acceptable. It's crucial to take a step back and unwind if you're feeling exhausted.

This can entail taking a day, a week, or even a month off from work. The most crucial thing is that you take the time to rest so that you can return to work with fresh vigor and focus.

Understanding the common challenges and obstacles that Etsy sellers face

Although starting and expanding a business can be difficult and rewarding, there are challenges to be faced. You could have a variety of typical difficulties as an Etsy vendor, which could harm your success. In this part, we'll look at some of the biggest challenges that Etsy sellers deal with and offer solutions.

The level of rivalry and saturation in a seller's niche is one of the major problems they encounter on Etsy. It can be challenging to stand out and draw customers given the platform's millions of vendors and products. It's crucial to carry out market research and comprehend your target audience if you want to overcome this difficulty. You may then develop a product line that is consistent with your brand and specialty by using this information to find lucrative niches and product trends. Using tags, keywords, and categories to make your products more visible will help you optimize your shop for search and exposure on Etsy.

Managing and overcoming burnout and stress is another difficulty faced by Etsy sellers. Running a business may be tough and time-consuming, especially in the beginning. To prevent burnout, it's critical to establish clear limits and give self-care a priority. It's crucial to effectively manage your time and automate procedures wherever you can.

Another typical problem for Etsy merchants is dealing with bad reviews and consumer complaints. Negative feedback can be damaging to your brand and reputation, but it's crucial to keep in mind that it can also be a chance to grow. It's critical to reply swiftly and professionally to negative feedback and complaints while also looking for methods to make things right for the customer.

It can be difficult to scale and manage your firm, especially as it expands. Setting clear objectives and expectations for your team is crucial when managing a team and allocating work. Additionally, it's critical to construct a system for measuring and tracking performance as well as an efficient communication system.

Finally, it can be difficult for Etsy sellers to comprehend and follow tax rules. Maintaining proper records of your income and expenses as well as staying up to speed on the tax rules and regulations that apply to your business are essential.

These are only a few of the issues that Etsy sellers frequently deal with, but you can position yourself for success on the marketplace by being aware of and ready for them. Keep an open mind, be willing to adjust, be informed, and ask for assistance when necessary. You are capable of creating a prosperous Etsy business if you have the correct perspective and tactics in place.

Tips for handling negative reviews and customer complaints in a professional and positive way

You will undoubtedly encounter unfavorable consumer feedback or complaints as an Etsy seller. But it's crucial to keep in mind that these instances are chances for your company to develop and learn. Here are some pointers for responding professionally and effectively to bad reviews and client complaints:

- Respond promptly: It's crucial to respond as soon as you can to a poor review or consumer complaint. This demonstrates to the client that you value their complaints and are eager to put things right.
- Apologize and take responsibility: Even if you disagree with the customer's complaint, you should nevertheless accept responsibility for the incident and provide an apology. The customer will see that you are willing to talk to them and apologize as a result.
- Offer a solution: It's crucial to express regret and give a resolution to the client's issue. This might be a reimbursement, a product swap, or a discount coupon for subsequent purchases.

- Follow up: After you've offered a solution, it's important to follow up with the customer to make sure they are satisfied with the outcome. This shows that you truly care about their satisfaction and are committed to making things right.
- Learn from the experience: Negative reviews and customer complaints can be difficult to handle, but it's important to remember that they offer valuable insights into your business. Use these experiences to identify areas for improvement and make changes to your processes and products.
- Use the feedback to improve your business: If a customer has a specific complaint, try to understand the root cause of the problem and take steps to prevent similar issues from happening in the future.
- Keep things professional: Even if the customer is angry or upset, it's important to remain professional and respectful in your response.
- Take the conversation offline: If a customer is particularly upset or the issue is sensitive, it's best to take the conversation offline and continue it via email or phone. This allows you to have a more private and controlled conversation.
- Use a positive tone: Be sure to use a positive and upbeat tone when responding to negative reviews and complaints. This will help to keep the customer calm and show that you are willing to work with them to resolve the issue.

In order to preserve a positive reputation for your company and keep customers coming back for more, you should use the advice in this article to professionally and effectively respond to unfavorable reviews and customer complaints.

Strategies for dealing with competition and saturation in your niche

To begin with, it's crucial to carry out in-depth market research in order to comprehend your competitors. Examine their product offers, price, and marketing tactics. Examine what they are doing successfully and any potential market gaps you can address. Your own pricing, product development, and marketing initiatives can benefit from this information.

Next, pay attention to how to distinguish your brand and goods. This can be accomplished through creating a distinct and enduring brand image, giving a broad selection of high-quality items, and offering top-notch customer service. Additionally, to differentiate yourself from the competitors, think about carving yourself a specific specialty within your larger market.

Focusing on fostering relationships with your clients is another tactic. This can be accomplished by conversing with them on social media, providing them with individualized offers and discounts, and routinely collecting feedback. You can lessen the effect that rivalry has on your sales by establishing a devoted consumer base.

Lastly, think about increasing your sales outlets outside of Etsy. Creating your own website or using other online marketplaces are two examples of how to do this. You may reach more people and expand your revenue streams by diversifying your sales methods.

The appropriate mindset and approaches can help you get over difficulties like saturation and competitiveness that are common to all businesses. You may improve your chances of success on Etsy by carrying out in-depth market research, differentiating your brand and items, developing relationships with clients, and utilizing a variety of sales channels.

Understanding the importance of managing stress and burnout and how to prevent it

Even on a platform like Etsy, starting and operating a business may be a wonderful and gratifying experience, but it can also be stressful and exhausting. As a business owner, it's critical to recognize the value of caring for your physical and mental health.

To avoid burnout, it's important to set reasonable expectations for oneself as well as goals. This entails being realistic about how much you can actually do in a particular amount of time and refraining from taking on more than you can handle. Setting boundaries between work and personal time and putting self-care first can both be beneficial.

The presence of a support network is crucial for preventing burnout. This can include close friends, relatives, and other business owners who are aware of the particular difficulties you are experiencing. Joining a community or group of people who share your interests can also offer important support and inspiration.

The strain of being dependent on a single platform or cash source might be lessened by diversifying your income streams. This can entail entering new markets, launching a website, or providing services in addition to products.

Managing competition and niche saturation is a regular difficulty for Etsy sellers. Having a strong brand and distinctive value proposition is one method to stand out. This may entail a distinct brand statement, distinctive product offerings, and a unified aesthetic.

By offering outstanding customer service, you may set yourself apart from the competition. This may involve prompt and tailored communication, providing warranties or guarantees, and going above and above to satisfy customers.

Finally, it's critical to stay current on the most recent approaches to search engine optimization and marketing, as well as industry trends. This might assist you in maintaining an edge over the competition and boosting sales.

It takes a combination of self-awareness, setting realistic goals, developing a support network, diversifying your income sources, building a strong brand, offering exceptional customer service, and keeping up with industry trends to prevent burnout, manage stress, and deal with competition and saturation in your niche.

Tips for maintaining a positive mindset and staying motivated

Although opening and operating an Etsy shop can be a tremendously exciting and rewarding experience, it also has its own unique set of difficulties and difficulties. Dealing with competition and saturation in their market is one of the biggest obstacles that Etsy merchants confront. It can be challenging to stand out and draw clients because there are so many stores and products accessible on the marketplace. However, you may overcome this obstacle and expand your business with the appropriate approaches and techniques.

Staying true to your brand and niche is one of the most crucial things to keep in mind when dealing with competition. Focus on high-lighting your distinctive selling propositions and the features that make your products stand out rather than attempting to directly compete with other merchants. This can be the premium materials you employ, the distinctive designs, or the top-notch customer service you offer.

Maintaining a current understanding of the newest trends and consumer preferences in your industry is another essential tactic for overcoming competition. By doing so, you can make sure that your offers are always pertinent and in demand as well as spot opportunities for new goods and services.

Managing stress and burnout is a crucial component of running a successful Etsy business. It's simple to become overburdened by the ongoing duties of running a business as your shop expands. For this reason, it's crucial to prioritize taking care of your physical and emotional health. Be careful you get adequate sleep, eat healthy, and take regular breaks. Setting reasonable expectations and goals for your company and for yourself is also crucial.

Delegating work to others is one strategy for coping with stress and burnout. It's crucial to assemble a team you can count on to assist you in running your company on a daily basis. This may entail taking on workers, using virtual assistants, or delegating work to independent contractors. You can make sure that your shop runs smoothly even when you can't be present by assigning duties and leading a crew.

Taking the time to focus on yourself is a crucial tactic for over-coming stress and burnout. This might entail engaging in activities like yoga classes, walks, or meditation. Make sure you're engaging in activities that allow you to unwind and recharge, whatever they may be.

Finally, it's critical to keep a positive outlook and remain motivated. Setting specific goals for your company and yourself, and then moving steadily toward achieving those goals, is one of the most efficient methods to achieve this. This could entail activities like drafting a business plan, deciding on financial objectives, or coming up with a marketing plan.

How to create a support system for yourself and your business

To assist you negotiate the ups and downs of being an entrepreneur, it's critical to realize the value of building a support system for both you and your company.

In order to construct a support system, it's important to establish a network of people who share your interests and who can provide you with direction and assistance. Joining online forums or organizations for Etsy merchants can be a terrific way to meet people who are familiar with the particular difficulties of operating an online store. It's also critical to look for mentoring or mentorship from more seasoned sellers or business owners.

Taking care of your physical and emotional health is another crucial component of building a support network. It's simple to become preoccupied with day-to-day business operations and overlook your personal wellbeing. Making time for regular exercise, a balanced diet, and sound sleep is crucial. It's also crucial to make time for the interests and pursuits that make you happy and relax.

Giving others chores and responsibilities is another approach to build a support network. It could become challenging to manage all of the duties on your own as your organization expands. You can reduce your workload and free up more time by hiring a virtual assistant or outsourcing some of the work, allowing you to concentrate on the projects that call for your specialized knowledge and abilities.

Finally, it's critical to have a strategy in place in case things don't work out as expected. Having a support network in place can assist you in getting through challenging times, whether they are caused by a personal setback or a period of slow sales. It's crucial to have a strategy in place in case things don't go according to schedule and to understand when to seek for assistance.

Understanding the importance of self-care and how to prioritize it

The act of looking after your physical, mental, and emotional health in order to enhance your general well being is known as self-care. Exercise, a healthy diet, getting adequate sleep, and participating in hobbies or enjoyable activities are a few examples of what it can entail. Making self-care a priority will help you manage the responsibilities of running a business and make smarter decisions.

Making time in your day for self-care is one way to prioritize it. This may be as easy as scheduling 30 minutes of exercise or meditation in the morning, or taking a break in the middle of the day to go for a stroll or have a healthy lunch. Setting limits and making time for yourself outside of work are equally vital. It can entail having a defined time each day to stop working or taking a day off each week to unwind and rejuvenate.

Creating a support network for oneself is another approach to place a high priority on self-care. This might involve close friends and family members as well as other business owners who can provide guidance and support in your personal life. Another excellent option to meet people who are familiar with the particular difficulties of running a business is to join a networking or business organization.

It's also crucial to pay attention to your mental and emotional wellbeing. To recognize and resolve any unfavorable thoughts or feelings that might be affecting your wellbeing, practice mindfulness and self-reflection. If necessary, speak with a therapist or counselor.

Remember that managing a business requires a lot of labor, and that you must look after yourself in order to advance and meet your objectives. Setting self-care as a priority will enhance both your health and the success of your business.

How to create a plan for dealing with unexpected challenges and obstacles

Identify potential challenges: You must first identify the potential challenges before you can develop a strategy to address them. Think about topics like shifting market conditions, shifting customer behavior, and shifting economic conditions. Consider the potential effects of these changes on your company and what you can do to lessen any negative effects.

Assess your vulnerabilities: Once you've discovered prospective difficulties, carefully examine your company to identify any potential weak points. For example, cash flow, inventory, or customer service could all be affected. Knowing your weaknesses will enable you to concentrate your efforts on the areas that require the greatest attention.

Develop a strategy: It's time to create a plan of action for addressing the issues after you've determined their potential and evaluated your vulnerabilities. Your plan should specify the particular measures you'll take to lessen the challenge's impact and the procedures you'll take to recover from it.

Create a plan of action: It's time to develop a plan of action now that your strategy is in place. This should outline specific tasks, deadlines, and completion dates that will keep you on track and help you reach your objectives.

Review and update your plan regularly: You should regularly evaluate and update your strategy as it should be a dynamic document. Your plan should evolve as your company does as it grows and evolves. It's critical to maintain flexibility and modify your plan as necessary to account for shifts in your industry and the general marketplace.

Tips for maintaining a work-life balance

Your wellbeing and the success of your business depend on you being able to strike a healthy work-life balance. Here are some pointers for keeping work and personal life in balance:

- Set boundaries. Clearly define the boundaries between work and personal time. This can involve setting apart particular times to check and reply to messages, allocating time specifically for spending time with family and friends, and planning regular breaks throughout the day.
- Prioritize self-care. Make sure you give self-care pursuits, like exercise, meditation, or a hobby, top priority. When you engage in these activities, you can unwind and recharge, which will improve your attention and productivity at work.
- Create a schedule. You can stay organized and use your time more effectively if you follow a routine. Establish a timetable that allows for time for work, self-care, and private pursuits.
- Communicate with your loved ones. Be careful to let your loved ones know how much time and effort you put into running your business. It may aid in their comprehension and support of your objectives.
- Seek help if needed. Never be embarrassed to seek friends and relatives for assistance. Having a support system may be quite beneficial, whether it is assistance with childcare, housework, or running errands.
- Learn to say no. Learn to say "no" to requests that conflict with your priorities or aspirations. This can assist you in maintaining your attention on what matters while avoiding overcommitting.

Do not forget that managing an Etsy store requires endurance, not haste. It's critical to look after both your professional and personal lives in addition to your business. You may create a healthy work-life balance and be more successful in the long run by setting boundaries, giving yourself priority, developing a timetable, connecting with loved ones, asking for help when necessary, and learning to say no.

Strategies for keeping yourself and your business resilient in the face of adversity.

It's critical to be ready for any difficulties that can come as an Etsy merchant. Making a strategy for handling unforeseen circumstances is one method to achieve this. This can involve making a support network of friends, family, or other business owners who can provide direction and advise, as well as scheduling a particular amount of time each week to reflect on your company and identify any problems.

Keeping a positive outlook is another crucial component of running a strong firm. This can be done by prioritizing the things that make you happy and fulfilled and having clear goals and priorities. It's crucial to prioritize your health and engage in self-care. This can involve scheduling time for leisure pursuits, physical activity, and rest, as well as ensuring that you get enough sleep and eat well.

The ability to balance work and personal obligations is essential for avoiding stress and burnout. This can be accomplished by clearly defining boundaries between work and personal time and by figuring out how to incorporate your interests and passions into your business. It's also crucial to pay attention to how much time and effort you are investing in your business and to modify as necessary to avoid overworking yourself.

Additionally, it's critical to understand the level of competition and market saturation in your specialty on Etsy. Investigating your competitors' products and the market on a regular basis is one approach to achieve this. You can use this to find out where you can make your items, prices, and marketing plan better. It's also critical to vary your product offering and concentrate on developing exceptional products that outperform the competition.

9

ADVANCED STRATEGIES FOR INCREASING REVENUE

Maximizing profit by understanding your target customer and optimizing your pricing

In order to maximize profit as an Etsy seller, it's critical to have a fantastic product as well as an understanding of your target market and pricing strategy.

Prior to anything else, it's critical to have a solid understanding of your target market. Finding out about their hobbies, demographics, and problems is necessary. Your product and marketing efforts can be tailored to your target market once you have a firm idea of who they are.

Next, in order to price your things properly, it's critical to comprehend your charges and expenses. This covers all associated costs, such as those for shipping and packaging in addition to the price of the materials and the cost of manufacturing. It's critical to establish a pricing that not only covers your expenses but also leaves room for profit.

It's crucial to take into account pricing and competition in your area. Check out comparable products to see what the market price is. This doesn't imply that you must match the competition, but it is crucial to comprehend the market and pricing patterns.

Offering a variety of pricing options, such as a free and paid version of your product, is one efficient pricing technique. This enables customers who are both price-conscious and prepared to spend extra. Consider discounting and bundling your products to get buyers to buy more than one.

Additionally, it's crucial to continually evaluate and modify your pricing plan as necessary. This entails monitoring your own sales and profit margins as well as those of your competitors and market trends.

Leveraging upselling and cross-selling to increase average order value

After you have a firm grasp on your ideal client, you can set rates that are both competitive for your industry and enable you to turn a profit. To further boost your profit margins, you can experiment with various price methods like providing bulk discounts, package discounts, or unique promotions.

Utilizing upselling and cross-selling is another efficient method for increasing profit. When you recommend customers buy a more expensive or upgraded version of the product they are now contemplating, this is known as upselling. Contrarily, cross-selling is when you recommend things that go well with the one the buyer is contemplating. You may raise the average order value and boost your company's revenue by utilizing these techniques.

For instance, you may upsell a customer who is considering purchasing a handmade clay mug by offering them a matching set of mugs or a larger size. Additionally, you might cross-sell by offering related goods like a pottery mug warmer or holder.

The suggested items must be pertinent to the customer's needs and interests when using upselling and cross-selling methods, and they must be presented in a non-pushy and professional manner. Additionally, make sure the things you recommend can be delivered promptly and are of a high caliber.

Utilizing data and analytics to make informed business decisions

Knowing your target audience is one of the main advantages of using data and analytics. You can obtain a better knowledge of your customers and what they are looking for by evaluating data such as customer demographics, purchase history, and browsing behavior. The demands and preferences of your target market can be better served by tailoring your marketing initiatives, product offers, and pricing approach.

Utilizing data and analytics to enhance your price is a crucial component. You may choose the best pricing points for your products by examining statistics such as sales, costs, and market trends. By doing this, you may raise your profit margins and maintain your position as a market leader. In order to keep on top of the game, you can also analyze market trends and industry benchmarks and alter your pricing strategy as necessary.

Powerful strategies that can be utilized to raise the average order value and optimize profit include upselling and cross-selling. At the time of sale, you can encourage customers to spend more money by recommending related or complimentary goods. Additionally, you can entice clients to buy more items by providing bundles or reduced packages.

A system for monitoring and measuring performance must be in place in order to use data and analytics effectively. This may involve using programs like Google Analytics, which can offer insightful data on website traffic and consumer behavior. Furthermore, Etsy has its own analytics tools, such as the "Shop Manager," which lets you view your sales, earnings, and customer information.

Finally, it's critical to routinely evaluate and analyze your data in order to spot trends, patterns, and areas that may be improved. This can involve observing consumer behavior to discover areas of your store that may be causing friction or confusion and evaluating sales data to determine your best-selling products and most lucrative customer segments. You may make wise business decisions that will assist to optimize your store and boost sales by frequently evaluating and analyzing data.

Understanding the importance of understanding your target customer and how to use that knowledge to optimize pricing

Making a customer persona is one method of determining who your target customer is. Based on data and research, a customer persona is a fictitious depiction of your ideal client. It ought to contain details like demographics, problems, and purchasing patterns. You may utilize this knowledge to decide on your items, price, and promotion once you have a firm understanding of your target market.

When it comes to pricing, it's crucial to take into account the costs of labor and materials as well as the costs of competing goods. The worth that your customers assign to your product—its perceived value—should also be taken into account. A handmade, unique object, for instance, might sell for more money than a mass-produced one.

Understanding price psychology is also crucial. Prices that finish in.99, for instance, are frequently thought of as being less expensive than those that end in.00. Offering discounts or package packages can also help your products appear to be a better value.

Upselling and cross-selling are two additional strategies for increasing profit. Upselling refers to the practice of persuading clients to buy a more expensive model of a product they are presently considering. When you cross-sell, you make recommendations for additional goods that go well with the item they're currently contemplating. For instance, you could recommend a matching hat or scarf if a customer is buying a hand-knit sweater.

Finally, using data and analytics is essential for producing business decisions that are well-informed. Understanding your sales data, consumer behavior, and market trends are all part of this. You may make judgments about your items, pricing, and marketing by evaluating this data to find patterns and trends.

A variety of analytics tools are available on Etsy, such as the shop stats page, which lets you monitor sales, views, consumer activity, and the effectiveness of your listing. You can then make the necessary adjustments after learning what is and is not working well.

You can take actions to maximize profit and expand your Etsy business by comprehending your target market, adjusting your price, upselling and cross-selling, and using data and analytics.

Techniques for leveraging upselling and cross-selling to increase average order value

The act of persuading clients to buy a more expensive or upgraded version of a product they are now evaluating is known as upselling. If a consumer is considering a basic t-shirt, for instance, you may propose a premium model with extra features like increased softness or a distinctive design.

Contrarily, cross-selling entails advising the client on related goods. You might advise matching earrings or a bracelet if a customer is purchasing a necklace, for instance.

It is possible to upsell and cross-sell in a tactful and non-obtrusive manner. For instance, in your product listing or follow-up emails, you can use expressions like "complete the look" or "customers who bought this also bought."

Understanding your target market and their wants is also crucial since it will enable you to choose the right products to offer as upsells or cross-sells. Using data and analytics to do market research and gain important insights into consumer preferences and purchasing trends.

To make sure that you are not only turning a profit but also that your rates are competitive in the market, it's also crucial to optimize your pricing. Track your sales using data and analytics, identify the sweet spot for pricing, and think about using discounts and promotions to boost sales.

Tips for using data and analytics to make informed business decisions

Conducting market research and comparing your rates to those of like products in your niche is a key strategy for pricing optimization. This can assist you in selecting a price that is both competitive and likely to generate sales.

Utilizing upselling and cross-selling is another method for

increasing profit. Cross-selling is the act of recommending related items that the consumer may also be interested in, whereas upselling is the process of persuading customers to buy an upgraded or higher-end version of the product they are currently interested in.

For instance, if a customer is buying a handcrafted notebook, you may cross-sell them a set of matching pens or upsell them by offering a deluxe version of the notebook with extra features. You may raise the average order value and enhance your revenue by using these strategies.

It's crucial to comprehend your target audience in addition to using data and analytics to create wise commercial judgments. You may spot patterns, trends, and opportunities for improvement by keeping an eye on your sales data and consumer behavior.

For merchants, Etsy offers a variety of analytics tools, such as the Purchases and Traffic Dashboard, which lets you monitor sales and view consumer information. You may learn what products are doing well, what marketing tactics are effective, and where you might need to make changes by constantly examining this data.

Additionally, you may watch the traffic to your website and acquire more specific data about the behavior of your customers using third-party analytics solutions.

How to use customer data to create personalized marketing campaigns

Understanding your target consumer is essential for expanding your Etsy business. You may tailor your pricing and product offers to better match your customers' demands and boost sales by getting to know their demographics, preferences, and behavior. Analyzing consumer information from your Etsy store, like purchase history and browsing habits, is one way to collect this data.

You may develop tailored marketing efforts if you have a thorough grasp of your target customer. For instance, if you see that the bulk of your clients are young mothers, you may design a campaign that explicitly targets that group and features goods that would be of interest to them, such baby clothes or nursery décor. It has been demonstrated that personalized marketing initiatives are more successful at increasing sales and cultivating consumer loyalty.

Upselling and cross-selling are two additional ways to boost revenues. The technique of persuading clients to buy a more expensive or upgraded version of the product they are presently evaluating is known as upselling. Contrarily, cross-selling is the technique of suggesting related products to customers based on their recent purchase. For instance, you might advise a customer buying a garment to accessorize it with a matching necklace or pair of earrings. You can raise the average order value and enhance revenue by employing cross- and up-selling strategies.

Analytical data and data-driven decision-making are crucial for commercial decision-making. Several analytics tools are available on Etsy that may be used to monitor sales, client behavior, and shop performance. You may learn patterns and trends from this data analysis and use them to guide your marketing and product development plans. Additionally, you can monitor website traffic and user behavior on your website or social media platforms using third-party analytics tools like Google Analytics.

Understanding the importance of testing and experimentation in optimizing pricing and product offerings

A/B testing is one method of testing and experimenting. This entails developing two distinct iterations of a pricing or product listing approach, comparing the outcomes, and determining which one performs better. This can be accomplished by little adjustments, like as altering product descriptions or prices, or major ones, like the introduction of a new product or a shift in your target market.

Surveys and focus groups are another technique to test and experiment. This enables you to acquire immediate customer input and comprehend their demands and preferences. This might assist you in determining where your pricing and product offerings need to be improved.

Additionally, it's crucial to remember that testing and experimentation should be ongoing processes. Your product offers and pricing should adapt as the market and consumer preferences do. You can stay ahead of the curve and continuously enhance your business by regularly testing and experimenting.

Making educated business decisions can be aided by using data and analytics in addition to testing and experimentation. You may learn what is and is not working by monitoring important indicators like sales, consumer behavior, and engagement. Following that, decisions about pricing, product offerings, and marketing tactics can be made using the information.

Tips for creating a culture of data-driven decision making within your business

For long-term success, it is essential to instill a culture of data-driven decision making within your company. You may better satisfy the demands of your target customers by optimizing pricing, product offers, and marketing efforts by using data and analytics to make informed decisions. Here are some guidelines for fostering a tradition of data-driven decision-making in your company:

- Start by determining the crucial performance indicators for your company. These could include figures like average order value, customer lifetime value, and cost of customer acquisition.
- Create a mechanism for routinely monitoring and analyzing these indicators. This can entail utilizing programs like Google Analytics or the analytics platform from Etsy.
- Encourage your team to make decisions based on data and analytics. This can entail organizing frequent meetings to talk about important KPIs and how to use them to advance the company.
- Establish a culture of testing and experimentation. Encourage your team to test various product offerings, pricing tactics, and marketing strategies to determine what is most effective.

- Personalized marketing campaigns can be created using data and analytics. You can improve the efficiency of your marketing campaigns and boost sales by segmenting your consumer base and focusing your marketing efforts on particular demographics.
- Make data-driven decisions a part of the culture and values of your business. Encourage everyone, from senior management to entry-level employees, to take data into account when making choices.
- To assist your team members in using data and analytics, provide training and resources. This can entail attending workshops, taking online courses, or even hiring a consultant or data analyst.

Understanding the importance of customer lifetime value and how to increase it

The overall revenue that a client will bring in for your company over the course of their lifetime is known as customer lifetime value (CLV). It is an important indicator to take into account as it can assist you determine the long-term worth of each customer and can guide your customer acquisition and retention tactics.

By providing outstanding customer service, you can raise CLV. This include answering customer questions as soon as they come in, taking care of any problems or complaints, and going above and beyond to satisfy them. You may boost the likelihood of recurring business and positive word-of-mouth recommendations by cultivating a base of devoted customers.

Implementing upselling and cross-selling strategies is another strategy to boost CLV. When you give them a more expensive or improved version of a product they are already interested in, this is known as upselling. Offering customers items that are complementary to the one they are already interested in is known as cross-selling. You may raise the average order value and improve income from each customer by providing these choices.

Additionally, you may track consumer behavior and look for cross-

and up-selling opportunities using data and analytics. You can learn about a customer's tastes and purchasing behavior by looking at their past purchases, and you can then utilize that knowledge to provide them with individualized recommendations.

Offering loyalty or referral programs is another tactic to raise CLV. You may boost the possibility of recurring business and draw in new customers by rewarding clients who make repeat purchases or refer friends and family.

Last but not least, it's critical to comprehend that CLV is not a constant and might alter over time. You can comprehend the changes in CLV and modify your tactics as necessary by routinely monitoring and analyzing customer data. You may raise CLV and promote long-term growth for your Etsy business by putting an emphasis on customer service, upselling and cross-selling, data and analytics, and loyalty programs.

Techniques for using data and analytics to optimize your marketing and advertising efforts

Client lifetime value, or the total sum of money a customer is antici-pated to spend with your organization during their lifetime, is a crucial metric to take into account. You can guarantee your company's long-term profitability and survival by raising customer lifetime value.

Upselling and cross-selling are two strategies for boosting customer lifetime value. You may raise the overall value of each transaction by providing customers with related or complimentary products while they are making a purchase. For instance, you may sell a scarf or hat to go with a hand-knit sweater the consumer is buying as an add-on.

Personalizing marketing initiatives is another strategy to raise customer lifetime value. You can improve the relevancy and efficiency of your campaigns by segmenting your consumer base and focusing your marketing messaging on particular audiences. This can be done by developing targeted email campaigns, social media adverts, and other marketing materials using client information such as purchase history and browsing behavior.

Utilizing data and analytics to improve your pricing approach is also crucial. To determine the sweet spot for your items, you can use statistics such as sales data, rival pricing, and customer feedback. After you choose the right price, you should keep testing and experimenting with different pricing plans to see which one is most effective for your company.

You should set up specific objectives and metrics that your team can monitor in order to foster a culture of data-driven decision making within your organization. Ensure that each member of your team is aware of these objectives and knows how they relate to the overall success of your company. Additionally, it's crucial to spend money on the correct equipment and technology to facilitate the collection, analysis, and interpretation of data.

Tips for using data to identify opportunities for business expansion.

Understanding your customer lifetime value is a crucial component of data analysis (CLV). The entire value a client will contribute to your company over the course of their lifetime is determined by the CLV measure. This covers not only the first purchase they make but also any subsequent purchases, recommendations, and other types of value they might provide. The entire profitability of your organization might be raised by comprehending and raising your CLV.

Utilizing data and analytics to optimize your pricing is one strategy to raise CLV. You may determine the sweet spot for your pricing by examining data on consumer demographics, purchasing patterns, and market trends. This price point should be neither too high nor too low to leave money on the table. Data can also be used to compare the performance of various pricing techniques, including dynamic pricing.

Through cross-selling and upselling, CLV can also be raised. You may raise the value of each transaction and promote recurring business by selecting additional goods or services that go well with a customer's original purchase. If a consumer buys a dress from your store, for instance, you may offer matching accessories or a garment of a similar design in a different color.

Your marketing and advertising activities can be optimized with the use of data and analytics. You can determine which campaigns and distribution channels are the most successful by monitoring their performance and allocating your resources accordingly. Additionally, you may segment your audience using data and develop customized marketing campaigns that cater to the preferences and demands of various client segments.

Finally, data and analytics can assist you in locating potential business growth prospects. For instance, you can learn by studying customer demographic data that a sizable share of your clientele is based in a particular region or is of a particular age. This could be a sign that there is a need for your goods or services in that region or among those people, and it may be a good time to grow your company.

10

CONCLUSION: ACHIEVING ETSY SUCCESS AND BEYOND

Reflecting on the journey and what you've learned

The lessons you've learnt are one of the first things to take into account when looking back on your trip. Consider what you've discovered regarding your target market, your product line, your marketing tactics, and any other aspects of your organization. Determine the elements that succeeded and those that failed. You'll be able to make wiser selections going forward thanks to this.

Your business goals and the progress you've made toward them are a crucial area to consider. Examine your development to determine whether you are making progress toward your objectives or whether there is room for improvement. You may keep moving toward achieving your long-term goals by taking stock of your development and making modifications as necessary.

It's crucial to reflect on the difficulties you've encountered and how you overcome them. You'll be more ready for difficulties in the future if you think back on the challenges you've encountered and the methods you used to conquer them.

Finally, it's critical to consider your whole journey and how you've developed as a person and a business owner. You'll have a greater understanding of the progress you've made and a sense of success by looking back on the journey. Additionally, it will assist you in making future plans and goal-setting.

Setting new goals and planning for continued growth

Although starting and expanding a business can be immensely gratifying, it also takes a lot of effort and commitment. It's vital to stop and think about what you've learned and how far you've come when you look back on your trip. This could be a wonderful chance to recognize your accomplishments and pinpoint areas that need work.

Your consumer base is among the most crucial factors to take into account when thinking back on your trip. What do your consumers want? Who are they? For your firm to be successful, you must comprehend your clients. It's also crucial to think about how your company has changed through time and how it will change moving forward.

The financial side of your business is another crucial factor to consider. Have you been successful in turning a profit? Are there any places where you could reduce expenses or raise money? For your company to keep expanding, it is essential that you understand your finances.

It's vital to think about the group that has supported you as you reflect on your trip. Recognizing the contributions of your staff is critical because they are a crucial component of your company. It's crucial to think about how your team can remain a useful asset in the future.

Finally, it's critical to consider your long-term objectives. What goals do you have for the upcoming year? 5-year period? A decade? For your company to develop and succeed, you must continually set new goals. When establishing these objectives and coming up with a strategy for reaching them, it's critical to be realistic and detailed.

Tips and resources for taking your business to the next level.

Starting and expanding a business may be both difficult and rewarding. It demands a significant amount of effort, dedication, and a readiness to change. To reflect on your journey thus far and the lessons you have learnt is one of the most crucial tasks in pushing your company to the next level. You can use this to pinpoint your areas for growth and create new objectives.

Evaluate your prior performance as one of the important aspects of reflection. Examine your sales and profit margins, client comments, and general company operations. Make a plan to deal with any areas where you could have performed better. This can involve things like stepping up your marketing initiatives, enhancing customer support, or optimizing your business procedures.

Setting new goals is a crucial next step in growing your company. This can entail things like boosting sales, broadening your product offering, or breaking into new markets. You must have a plan in place in order to accomplish these objectives. This can involve making a budget, coming up with a marketing plan, or employing more employees.

Leveraging data and analytics is one of the most efficient ways to accomplish your goals. You may use data to better understand your clients and spot opportunities, which will help you make decisions that will advance your company. You can use a variety of tools and resources to aid you with this, such as:

- Google Analytics: This is a free tool that can help you track website traffic, sales, and customer behavior.
- Excel or Google Sheets: These are spreadsheet programs that can be used to track and analyze data.
- Business intelligence software: These are specialized tools that can help you gain insights from your data and make better decisions.

Focusing on customer lifetime value is another essential tactic for growing your company. This entails putting equal emphasis on retaining existing clients as well as attracting new ones. This can involve things like delivering exceptional customer service, setting up a loyalty program, and offering unique discounts and promotions.

Finally, it's critical to establish a strategy for future expansion. For example, you might broaden your product offering, penetrate new markets, or create new revenue streams. You will need to be continually learning and adjusting to new opportunities and obstacles if you want to accomplish this. You can use online classes, mentoring programs, and networking events as some options to assist you with this.

A summary of the key concepts and strategies covered throughout the book

Prior to creating a product line that is consistent with your brand, it's critical to have a clear grasp of your brand and niche. To ensure the quality of the final product, this entails locating and selecting suppliers and materials as well as using methods like prototyping and testing. It's also essential to enhance the look and branding of your business, develop aesthetically appealing product listings with attention-grabbing titles and descriptions, and more.

Additionally essential to boosting sales on Etsy are marketing and promotion. This includes creating a following on social media, advertising on paid platforms, and employing influencer marketing and paid social media to promote your business and products. Making engaging email campaigns is essential if you want to use email marketing to increase sales. To make your business and products more visible on Etsy search, it's also crucial to apply SEO tactics.

Running an Etsy business also involves analyzing and controlling your expenditures, expenses, and taxes, as well as managing your inventory and fulfillment. Additionally, it's essential to use the analytics tools offered by Etsy to evaluate the success of your marketing and advertising activities and make data-driven decisions.

As your company expands, it's critical to diversify your product offering to boost sales, to outsource and automate tasks to boost productivity, and to lead and inspire a team. Understanding the value of scaling your business, establishing clear expectations for your staff, building up an efficient communication system, and monitoring and measuring success are also essential.

It's also critical to be aware of the typical difficulties and roadblocks that Etsy sellers have, like bad feedback and complaints from customers, competitiveness and market saturation in your specialty, stress and burnout, and competition. Making a strategy for overcoming unforeseen difficulties and hurdles, preserving a healthy work-life balance, and placing a high priority on self-care are all crucial.

Understanding your target consumer will help you optimize pricing, enhance average order value through upselling and cross-selling, and use data and analytics to make smart business decisions. It's crucial to leverage consumer data to develop targeted marketing campaigns, test and experiment with different pricing strategies, and use data to spot business growth prospects.

Finally, it's crucial to create new objectives and make plans for ongoing development as you think back on your trip. The possibilities are infinite if you have the correct attitude and the will to advance your company. There are many resources accessible to help.

Reflecting on your own journey and progress as an Etsy seller

Reviewing your previous sales information and client reviews is one approach to take stock of your trip. This can help you gain insight into the most well-liked products, what customers like and dislike about your goods, and the kinds of customers you tend to draw. This data can be used to spot patterns in your company, including seasonal variations in sales.

Examining your previous marketing and advertising efforts is another way to consider your journey. What tactics have been most successful in bringing customers and sales to your store? What tactics haven't been as effective? You can use this data to inform your future decisions on how to allocate your marketing budget.

It's crucial to take stock of your own development as a business owner. Have you picked up any new abilities or knowledge that will help your company? Have you grown more self-assured in your selling prowess? You might find places where you can still develop and improve by thinking back on your own personal development.

It's time to set new objectives and make plans for continued development after you've thought back on your path. This could entail improving your marketing efforts, diversifying your clientele, or growing your product line. Setting precise, quantifiable objectives that are consistent with your entire business vision is crucial.

There are numerous resources available to Etsy sellers to assist you in achieving your new objectives. For instance, the website Etsy provides a range of online workshops and classes on subjects including marketing, photography, and product creation. Additionally, you may share information with other business owners and ask for guidance in a variety of online groups for Etsy merchants.

In conclusion, taking stock of your experiences and development as an Etsy seller will help you pinpoint areas of success and places for development. You can keep expanding and developing your firm by setting new objectives and making use of the resources at your disposal. Never lose sight of your overarching goal and never stop aiming for excellence in every facet of your company.

Tips for setting new goals and planning for continued growth

It's time to set new goals after you have a thorough awareness of your existing circumstance. These objectives must to be clear, quantifiable, and doable. For instance, you might decide to expand your product line to cover a new category of goods or to grow your sales by 20% within the upcoming quarter.

It's crucial to have a plan in place if you want to accomplish your goals. This could involve finding new target customers, putting new marketing techniques into practice, or optimizing your company's processes. Additionally, it's critical to be adaptable, receptive to new chances as they present themselves, and constantly on the lookout for methods to advance and expand your company.

Keeping up with the most recent developments and industry best practices is another crucial component of sustained success. Maintaining relationships with other Etsy merchants in your neighborhood and participating in organizations or forums where you can gain insight from others' experiences are also wise moves. You can also benefit from the numerous online resources, including webinars, tutorials, and e-books.

Finally, it's critical to keep in mind that expanding a business requires time and effort. Even when development is sluggish, it's crucial to have patience and maintain motivation. Celebrate your accomplishments, no matter how modest, and try not to be too hard on yourself when things don't go according to plan.

Understanding the importance of continuing education and how to stay up-to-date with the latest trends and best practices

Checking the Etsy news page frequently, where upgrades and new features are released, is a good way to keep updated. Etsy also provides a variety of live and recorded webinars and workshops on a number of subjects, including photography, SEO, and social media marketing. These can be a fantastic way to expand your knowledge of the industry and learn new skills.

Joining online forums for Etsy sellers, such as Facebook groups, is another method to keep informed. These communities offer a forum for information exchange, question-asking, and networking with other sellers. Additionally, a lot of industry leaders and influencers have blogs and social media pages where they post advice on how to expand your Etsy shop. A fantastic approach to keep informed is to follow these people and read their articles.

Making connections with other Etsy vendors can be a great way to get advice and assistance. This can be accomplished by going to occasions like craft fairs and trade displays, as well as by taking part in meet-ups and networking groups.

Finally, it's crucial to always be willing to learn and experiment. This can entail trying out new product lines, marketing methods, or technologies to make your operations run more smoothly. To keep expanding and enhancing your business, it's important to remain flexible and open to trying new things.

How to take your Etsy business to the next level by expanding to other platforms or creating your own website

Making your own website is a common strategy for growing your business. You can add more features and functionality as a result, and you have total control over the look and feel of your online business.

Owning a website can also help you build your brand and gain more credibility with customers.

But it's crucial to think about the costs and resources needed to run your own website before making the plunge. It's also crucial to keep in mind that setting up and maintaining your own website might take some time and takes some technical expertise.

Selling on different online markets is another way to grow your business. A wonderful approach to reach a new audience is through marketplaces like Amazon Handcrafted, which sells only handmade goods. Walmart and eBay are two other well-known online markets.

It's crucial to investigate and evaluate each marketplace's costs, regulations, and clientele before considering expanding to another one. It's crucial to think about if the market fits your brand and offerings.

It's also crucial to remember that growing your business on other platforms does not entail neglecting your Etsy store. Maintaining and expanding your online presence on Etsy is crucial.

It's critical to keep up with the newest trends and best practices in e-commerce in addition to expanding to new platforms. This can be accomplished by reading trade journals and blogs, going to conferences and trade exhibitions, and networking with other sellers.

In conclusion, growing your business beyond Etsy and setting up your own website might be wonderful ways to advance it. It's crucial to take into account the expenses and resources needed, as well as whether the platform is compatible with your brand and offerings. Additionally, it's critical to maintain and expand your presence on Etsy as well as to keep up with the most recent e-commerce trends and best practices.

Tips for networking and building relationships with other Etsy sellers and industry experts

As an Etsy seller, networking and establishing connections with other sellers and business leaders may be extremely beneficial to your company. It can not only foster a sense of belonging and support, but it can also create chances for partnerships, cross-promotion, and industry trend analysis. Here are some pointers for creating and preserving connections in the Etsy community:

- Join and take part in forums and groups for Etsy sellers online. These are available on sites like Facebook and Reddit, and they may be a fantastic way to meet other merchants and exchange tips and guidance.
- Participate in live events and trade shows. Craft fairs and maker markets are just a couple of the events that many cities and regions host for Etsy vendors. These gatherings offer fantastic chances to connect with other sellers and industry leaders.
- Connect with other vendors and industry leaders through social media. Social media sites like Instagram and Twitter may be a terrific way to interact with the community, connect with other sellers, and showcase your work.
- Directly contact other merchants and industry professionals. Don't be hesitant to introduce yourself if there is a specific seller or expert whose work or advise you value. With these contacts, you never know what opportunities might present themselves.
- Be receptive to partnerships and collaborations. Working together with other vendors can be a wonderful approach to promote your company and provide your customers with distinctive and special goods.

You can acquire important information, support, and growth possibilities by establishing and sustaining relationships with other members of the Etsy community. Always act professionally, with respect, and in a way that helps your fellow sellers. This will help you become a well-respected member of the community and create chances for partnerships, networking, and mentoring.

Understanding the importance of innovation and how to stay ahead of the competition

In any industry, staying ahead of the competition is essential, and the Etsy marketplace is no different. It's critical for Etsy sellers to continuously search for new trends, items, and tactics that will set them apart from the competition. This not only helps you draw in new consumers but also encourages repeat business from your current clientele.

Staying inventive is one of the most crucial strategies to keep one step ahead of the competition. Innovation can take many different forms, including the creation of novel items, fresh approaches to marketing and product promotion, or distinctive brand experiences for your clients. The secret is to keep an open mind, remain curious, and always be on the lookout for methods to advance and develop your company.

Maintaining a current understanding of the most recent trends and industry best practices is another method to keep one step ahead of the competition. In order to improve your goods and services, you must keep up with new developments in technology, manufacturing, and business practices. In order to more effectively target your marketing and sales activities, it's also critical to stay up to date on changes in consumer behavior and demographics.

Maintaining an edge over the competition also requires networking and developing partnerships with other Etsy sellers and subject matter experts. You can gain knowledge from the experiences of other sellers and subject-matter experts, gain insightful information, and keep up with changes in your specialized field by connecting with them. Attend trade shows, become involved in online forums, and look for mentoring opportunities to expand your network and learn useful information.

Finally, it's critical to keep in mind that innovation involves not just developing new goods and services but also figuring out fresh and inventive ways to market and sell them. Try out several marketing tactics, such as social media campaigns, influencer alliances, and email marketing, and monitor your results to determine which is most effective.

In essence, staying ahead of the pack on Etsy calls for a blend of creativity, knowledge retention, networking and relationship development, and experimenting.

A list of resources and further reading for continuing your Etsy education

Understanding the value of continuing your education and staying current with the newest trends and best practices is crucial if you're an Etsy vendor. To assist you in expanding your Etsy business, check out the following resources and recommended reading:

- Etsy's Seller Handbook: This comprehensive guide covers everything from setting up your shop to marketing and promotion, and is a great resource for new and experienced sellers alike.
- The Etsy Blog: Stay up-to-date with the latest news, trends, and best practices by regularly reading the Etsy blog.
- Etsy Success: This monthly newsletter for Etsy sellers is packed with tips, strategies, and inspiration to help you grow your business.
- Etsy Teams: Joining an Etsy team is a great way to connect with other sellers in your niche and learn from their experiences.
- Social Media: Follow industry leaders and experts on social media platforms like Instagram, Twitter, and Facebook for inspiration and tips.
- Podcasts: There are many podcasts dedicated to the world of e-commerce and Etsy, such as the "Etsy Conversations" podcast, which features interviews with successful Etsy sellers and industry experts.
- Books: There are many books that can help you take your Etsy business to the next level, such as "The Handmade Entrepreneur" by Kari Chapin, "The Etsy Seller's Handbook" by Jason Malinak and "Etsy Empire" by Jason Miles and Allison Marsh.

- Conferences and Workshops: Attending conferences and workshops can help you stay up-to-date with the latest trends and best practices, as well as connect with other Etsy sellers and industry experts.

You may keep developing and enhancing your Etsy business by being informed and utilizing these resources. Keep in mind that there is always space for progress and growth when it comes to learning and staying informed.

A final call-to-action for readers to take the next step towards Etsy success.

Congratulations on reaching the end of this guide on building a successful Etsy business! We hope that the tips and strategies provided have given you a solid foundation to work from, and that you are feeling motivated and excited to take your business to the next level.

To truly achieve success on Etsy and continue growing your business, it is essential to stay up-to-date with the latest trends and best practices in the industry. One of the best ways to do this is by constantly seeking out new resources and furthering your education.

Innovation is also key to staying ahead of the competition. Keep an eye out for new and emerging trends in your niche, and consider experimenting with new products or marketing strategies.

Networking with other Etsy sellers and industry experts is also a great way to stay inspired and learn from others who have found success on the platform.

Expanding to other platforms or creating your own website can also be a great way to take your business to the next level. This will give you more control over your brand and customer experience, and also opens up new opportunities for marketing and promotion.

Thanks for reading and best of luck on your Etsy journey! Remember, the key to success is to continuously learn, grow and adapt. Keep pushing yourself and your business forward, and you'll be sure to achieve the success you desire.